HARPSICHORD

Design and Construction

HARPSICHORD

Design and Construction

Evan J. Kern

VAN NOSTRAND REINHOLD COMPANY
NEW YORK CINCINNATI TORONTO LONDON MELBOURNE

Printed in The United States of America
Designed by Loudan Enterprises

Published by Van Nostrand Reinhold Company
A division of Litton Educational Publishing, Inc.
135 West 50th Street, New York, NY 10020, U.S.A.

Van Nostrand Reinhold Limited
1410 Birchmount Road
Scarborough, Ontario M1P 2E7, Canada

Van Nostrand Reinhold Australia Pty. Ltd.
17 Queen Street
Mitcham, Victoria 3132, Australia

Van Nostrand Reinhold Company Limited
Molly Millars Lane
Wokingham, Berkshire, England

16 15 14 13 12 11 10 9 8 7 6 5 4 3 2 1

Library of Congress Cataloging in Publication Data

Kern, Evan J
  The harpsichord: design and construction.

  1. Harpsichord--Construction. I. Title.
ML651.K43   786.2'3   79-22476
ISBN 0-442-23348-5

To Lucy

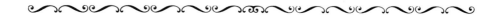

CONTENTS

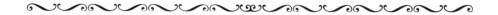

PREFACE

After almost two hundred years of neglect, there is a renewed interest in the harpsichord and its music. Harpsichord recitals are commonplace. Music students in conservatories and schools of music can pursue major studies in playing the harpsichord, and more and more people seek to own a harpsichord for their personal playing pleasure. This growth of interest in the harpsichord has led to considerable demand for the instrument.

Interestingly enough, there have been few successful attempts to meet this demand for the harpsichord through mass-production. The majority of the instruments being produced today are handcrafted in small shops scattered across the nation in much the same way they were produced in Europe two or more centuries ago. Because they are handcrafted, harpsichords are expensive instruments to own. Their cost ranges from several thousand dollars upward, effectively excluding them from many middle- and lower-income budgets. In addition, as a result of their being handcrafted, there usually is considerable waiting time between the ordering of a harpsichord and its delivery. Delays of four or five years are not uncommon.

As a consequence of the expense and time involved in the purchase of a harpsichord, many individuals have undertaken the construction of an instrument for their own use. In recognition of this interest, several companies now produce harpsichords in kit form that can be put together by an amateur with minimal experience, tools, and equipment. In the main, these kits are well designed, so much so that in some instances amateur builders have turned professional by selling the harpsichords they have constructed from these kits. As satisfactory as these kits are, however, there comes a time when many novice harpsichord-makers no longer are satisfied with putting together a pre-designed kit. They want to make decisions about such matters as compass, scale, size, and visual appearance; they want to exercise greater control over the final form and structure of the harpsichord.

Designing and constructing one's own harpsichord, however, is a very complex matter. Plans must be drawn, jacks must be designed and fabricated; the bent side must be laminated; the keyboard must be constructed; and the bridges must be pinned. Myriad details must be attended to before the instrument is completed. All of this designing and constructing requires considerable knowledge and skill that a novice harpsichord-maker could not be expected to possess, simply because such knowledge and skill grows out of extensive research and actual experience in designing and constructing harpsichords. It is apparent that some form of guidance is needed. This book has been written to provide that guidance.

PART I.

The Structure of the Harpsichord

The harpsichord can be described most simply as a mechanized lute, much the same as the organ can be described as a mechanized flute, and the piano as a mechanized hammer dulcimer. In the harpsichord, the keys serve as mechanical extensions of the player's fingers and actuate the mechanism that plucks the strings. The five elements essential to the operation of the harpsichord are (1) the strings, (2) the keyboard, (3) the jacks, (4) the bridges, and (5) the soundboard. All the other parts of the harpsichord are ancillary to these five.

1. *Action of the Jack*

A. Key Lever	F. String
B. Balance Rail	G. Nut
C. Jack Guide	H. Bridge
D. Jack Slide	I. Plectrum
E. Jack	J. Damper

2. *Plan View of Harpsichord*

A. Spine	F. Keyboard	K. Jack Slide
B. Tail	G. End Block	L. Soundboard
C. Bent Side	H. Name Board	M. Sound Hole
D. Short Side	I. Wrest Plank	N. Bridge
E. Lock Board	J. Nut	

As the player depresses the key (see Figure 1), the key pivots at its midpoint, causing the jack resting on the far end of the key to move upward past the string. The plectrum, a small piece of plastic, leather, or other material, projects from the upper part of the jack and plucks the string as it passes, causing the string to vibrate. The string is stretched between the bridges, one of which is fastened to the soundboard. The vibrations of the plucked string are transmitted through the bridge to the soundboard, which, in turn, amplifies the vibrations of the string so that they can be heard. As the player releases the key, the jack descends back past the string without plucking it (by means of a mechanism that will be described later). A small piece of felt attached to the upper part of the jack comes to rest on the string and effectively dampens its vibrations. This simple mechanism is duplicated for each key of the harpsichord. Obviously, keys, jacks, strings, bridges, and soundboard cannot simply float in space. Consequently, the key frame, sound box, harpsichord case, and other parts are necessary. A plan view and cross-sectional drawing of the harpsichord with each of these parts identified is given in Figures 2 and 3. The form and functions of these parts are discussed in detail in the sections that follow.

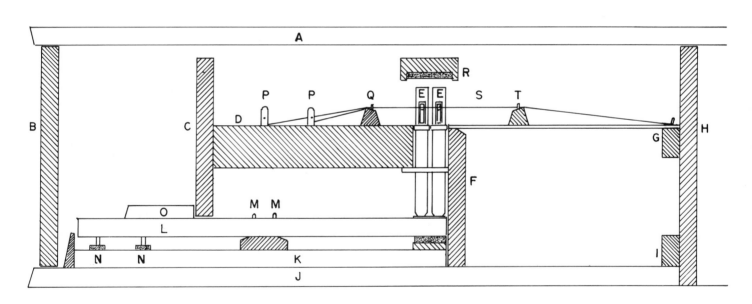

3. Cross Section of Square-cheeked Harpsichord

A. Lid	H. Spine	O. Accidental Comb
B. Removable Lock Board	I. Bottom Liner	P. Tuning Pin
C. Name Board	J. Bottom	Q. Nut
D. Wrest Plank	K. Key Frame	R. Jack Rail
E. Jack	L. Key	S. String
F. Belly Rail	M. Balance Rail Pin	T. Bridge
G. Hitch Pin Rail	N. Front Rail Pin	

The Strings

When a piece of music wire, such as the string on a harpsichord, is stretched between two points, it can be set in vibration simply by plucking the string at some point along its length. The plucked string will vibrate at a constant rate but at a steadily decreasing amplitude until eventually the vibrations of the string will cease completely. As the plucked string vibrates, it alternately compresses and rarifies the air surrounding it. These compressions and rarifications are called sound waves, which allow us to hear the vibrating string.

The strings of the harpsichord usually are made of steel or brass wire ranging in length from a few inches to six or more feet and in diameter from .008 inch or less to .025 inch or greater. In most harpsichords, the strings are plain wire; that is, they are not overspun or wrapped with another wire as are, for example, the bass strings on a guitar or a piano. Overspun strings are used only when an instrument has extremely short strings in the bass section or when the range of the instrument is extended a considerable distance down the scale.

The wire used for strings on the harpsichord is called music wire. The various sizes of music wire have been standardized, with the different diameters being identified by gauge numbers. The gauges and diameters apply to both steel and brass music wire. Table 1 lists the gauges and diameters of music wire commonly used in harpsichord construction.

The Physical Properties of Vibrating Strings.

The vibrating rate of a string is known as its frequency and is given in cycles per second (cps). Strings can be caused to vibrate over a wide range of frequencies, from the subsonic, through the audio range, and into the supersonic. The strings on a musical instrument are selected so that they vibrate at certain specified frequencies. These frequencies represent the various notes of the musical scale. Thus, a string that vibrates at 523.3 cps would produce the sound associated with c^2 (Pitch C), which is one octave above c^1 (Middle C) on the musical scale. (The English system of notation has been adopted for this book. See Appendix 1 for an explanation of this system.)

The frequency at which a string will vibrate is controlled by three factors. These factors are: (1) the length of the string, (2) the tension of the string, and (3) the mass of the string. These factors control the frequency of the string in the following ways:

Length: The shorter the string, the higher the vibrating frequency; the longer the string, the lower its vibrating frequency—providing the other two factors, tension and mass, remain constant.

Tension: The greater the tension, the higher the vibrating frequency; the lower the tension, the lower the vibrating frequency—providing the other two factors, length and mass, remain constant.

Mass: the smaller the mass, the higher the vibrating frequency; the larger the

---

TABLE 1

GAUGES, DIAMETERS, AND BREAKING POINTS OF MUSIC WIRE MEASURED BY THE AMERICAN STANDARD MUSIC WIRE GAUGE

Size	Diameter	Breaking point in pounds (Steel)	(Brass)	Approximate feet per pound
4/0	.006	8.5	3.0	10,204
3/0	.007	11.5	4.5	7,462
2/0	.008	15.0	6.0	5,714
0	.009	19.0	7.0	4,545
1	.010	23.5	9.0	3,700
2	.011	28.5	11.0	3,033
3	.012	34.0	13.0	2,560
4	.013	40.0	15.0	2,170
5	.014	46.0	18.0	1,886
6	.016	60.0	23.0	1,428
7	.018	76.0	29.0	1,136
8	.020	94.0	36.0	917
9	.022	114.0	44.0	757
10	.024	135.0	52.0	636
11	.026	159.0	61.0	540
12	.029	198.0	76.0	445

mass, the lower the vibrating frequency—providing the other two factors, length and tension, remain constant.

Because of the relationships of these three factors to the vibrating frequency of a string, it would seem that there is a wide latitude in the selection of strings for a musical instrument. In fact, however, there are limits to the variations in length, tension, and mass possible for producing a sound of a given frequency.

The limits on the practical length of a string for the harpsichord are attributable to the effect the length of a given string for a given note has on either the design or the sound of the instrument. For example, while a string 12 feet in length theoretically might produce the sound of the note GG, in practice it will be found that, when plucked, a string of such a length will vibrate so wildly as to clash against its neighbor and be almost impossible to dampen effectively. Moreover, there would be few places one could house a harpsichord with 12-foot strings. As to shortness, it is theoretically possible to have a string one-half-inch long that will sound the note g^3. Such a string will have little mass and, as a consequence, will produce sound waves of such small amplitudes as to be practically inaudible. Also, with such a short string, it would be almost impossible to fit the jacks and jack slides within the space between the two bridges. As a result, there are practical limits to the lengths of the strings used in the harpsichord.

The second factor, tension, refers to the stretching force exerted on the string, either by a weight (as in the science laboratory) or by a tensioning device, such as the tuning pin used in the harpsichord. Tension is measured either in pounds or in grams. Theoretically, it is possible for a string of a given size (length and mass) to vibrate at a given frequency with but a few pounds of tension. Also, it is theoretically possible for another string of a different size to vibrate at the same frequency with a tension of several hundred pounds. However, strings under low tension tend to be limp and lifeless, and when plucked, they produce a sound more noise-like than musical. And, as with strings of excessive length, strings under low tension tend to vibrate wildly and are difficult to control. On the other hand, strings with tension that is too great may impose excessive stress on the structure of the harpsichord, and, as a consequence, they may literally pull the instrument apart. Also, each gauge of music wire has a specific breaking point, a tension above which the string cannot be raised without breaking. Thus, as with length, there are practical limits to the tension for the strings of the harpsichord.

The third factor, mass, once again has practical limits that are imposed by the demands of the harpsichord. The mass of a string is its actual physical weight measured in pounds or grams. The mass of a string is determined by multiplying the density of the material used (normally given in pounds per cubic inch or grams per cubic centimeters) by the volume of the string (the cross-sectional area of the string multiplied by its length).

The mass of a string can be changed in several ways—first, through density. Different metals have different densities. Metals like gold and lead are quite dense (heavy), whereas metals like aluminum and magnesium are quite light. However, a string made of lead, while being comparatively heavy for a given length and diameter, has an extremely low breaking point and, even more important, totally lacks musical quality when plucked. The word "thud" would be apt to describe the sound of a lead string. A string made of a light metal, aluminum for example, has a low breaking point (but not as low as that of lead), and the sound of an aluminum string when plucked, while acoustically more interesting than that of a lead string, still leaves some musical qualities to be desired. As a practical solution to the matter of density, steel has been found to be the most successful metal for the strings of a harpsichord. A string made from steel is strong, heavy, and musical. Brass, a metal heavier than steel, also is used for harpsichord strings, especially in the bass section. However, the breaking point for a bass string is considerably lower than that of a steel string of the same diameter.

The second way to change the mass of a string is to change its length or diameter or both. Some of the limitations of this already have been discussed. In addition, though, it should be noted that, as a string increases in diameter in proportion to its length, it begins to lose its flexibility until, when the diameter becomes excessive, it no longer acts acoustically as a string but rather as a rod.

The third way to increase the mass of a given string without sacrificing flexibility, strength, or musical quality is to wrap a string of a given diameter with another wire, either of the same or a softer metal. Such strings are called ''overspun'' and are used extensively in such instruments as the piano, guitar, and violin. They have limited use in the harpsichord.

The designer of the musical instrument solves the string problems of length, tension, and mass empirically, that is, by determining what works best through experiment and experience. Experience has shown several things: (1) A string sounds best when it approaches its breaking point (however, some leeway must be allowed so that slight accidental overtightening or a minor binding of the string against the bridges or bridge pins does not result in breakage). (2) The closer all the strings are to the same tension, the more even they will sound throughout the compass of the harpsichord and the less the possibility for structural distortion of the instrument. (3) A string scale in which the length of the string for Pitch C is between 10 inches and 16 inches works best, with 13 inches being the most commonly accepted length. (The rest of the strings in the instrument are proportional to that chosen for Pitch C.) (4) Steel strings with diameters ranging from .009 inch for a 10-inch Pitch C, to .012 inch for a 14-inch Pitch C, and with .011 inch for a 12-inch Pitch C seem to be the most appropriate.

The point at which a harpsichord string is plucked also is a factor in determining the quality of the sound of the instrument. As the term indicates, the plucking point is that point on the string where the plectrum of the jack plucks. Up to a point, the closer the string is plucked to the bridge, the richer it will be in harmonics; however, when the string is plucked too close to the bridge, the sound becomes nasal and ''twangy.'' The closer to the mid-point the string is plucked, the fuller and cleaner will be the sound. The difference in the sound qualities of the various plucking points is because the partials, which are present at the plucking point, are canceled by the plucking action. (The term ''partials'' refers to the complex of frequencies heard when a string is plucked. The lowest of these partials is known as the fundamental. The rest are overtones. Harmonics are overtones that are multiples of the fundamental. Thus the second harmonic vibrates at twice the frequency of the fundamental, the fourth harmonic at four times the rate of the fundamental, etc.) Therefore, when a string is plucked in the middle, both the second and fourth harmonics are lost; when the string is plucked at one-seventh of its length, only the seventh harmonic is lost. Consequently, the point at which a string is plucked is of fundamental importance to its tonal color.

Because the seventh harmonic is musically the most objectionable overtone produced by a vibrating string, it is desirable to eliminate this harmonic. In the ideal harpsichord string plan, the plucking point is arranged so that it will fall at exactly one-seventh the length of each string. In practice, however, this ideal cannot be achieved. In the treble section, there simply is not sufficient space available to place each jack at a point one-seventh the length of the string it plucks; in the bass section, the plucking of a string at one-seventh of its length will require a key of excessive length. Consequently, in actual practice the plucking point in the treble approaches more nearly one-third to one-half the length of the string and, in the bass, about one-tenth the length of the string.

Also of importance in this discussion of the plucking of the strings is the disposition of the jacks—the orientation of the jacks in relation to the strings they pluck. For a harpsichord with multiple sets of strings, some of the jacks controlled by a given key will pluck the strings that are on the treble side of the jacks, and the remaining jacks will pluck the strings on the bass side. Selecting which set of jacks will pluck which set of strings can make considerable difference in the tonal color of a harpsichord. From the foregoing, it is obvious that the string plucked by the jack closest to the nut will be richer in harmonics than the one plucked farthest from the nut. To further complicate matters, the two unison strings assigned to any one note, actually will have two different vibrating lengths, although they will vibrate at exactly the same frequency, thus the term unison. This difference in length is due to the constantly changing bridge and nut centerlines brought about by the continual lengthening of strings from one note to another. Consequently, each string, when plucked, will sound differently than the other, so much so that the same harpsichord played with one disposition will sound entirely different when played with another disposition.

The objective in selecting an appropriate disposition for the jacks is to obtain the widest tonal color possible. Thus, with a harpsichord carrying two unisons, this will be achieved by having the farthest rank of jacks pluck to the right, or treble, side and the nearer rank of jacks pluck to the left, or bass, side. When the instrument has an eight-foot and a four-foot set of strings, it is customary to place the eight-foot jacks nearest the keyboard and have them pluck to the left, since this will align the jacks more closely to the one-seventh position. The four-foot strings, since their bridge is closer to the ranks of jacks, will sound best when plucked to the

right by the jacks in the back rank. When the harpsichord has two eight-foot and one four-foot set of strings, the recommended disposition is to place the four-foot rank of jacks between the two eight-foot ranks. This provides the greatest tonal differences between the two eight-foot ranks and, thus, increases the total expressiveness of the instrument.

The Compass of the Harpsichord. The compass of the instrument refers to the range of tones available within the capacity of the harpsichord. Since different registrations will affect the range of tones available, it is customary to give the compass of an instrument in terms of the eight-foot stop. Historically, the compass of the harpsichord has varied considerably. In a survey of three works on the harpsichord (see Bibliography, references 1,2, and 3), CC was found to be the lowest note and A the highest note of the last key in the bass section of any instrument. Also, a^3 was found to be the highest note and a^2 the lowest note of the last key in the treble section of any instrument. Table 2 reveals the many different compasses found in existing harpsichords. In this same survey, the most frequently found compasses in modern harpsichords were: FF to f^3, AA to f^3, FF to g^3, and C to f^3. The choice of compass is a choice of the desired range of music to be played on the instrument. Any one of the first three compasses given above is appropriate for music of the late Baroque period, with the exception of some Scarlatti sonatas, and onward. The fourth compass, C to f^3, represents that of the more lightly strung Italian harpsichord and will not encompass some of the music of the late Baroque period.

TABLE 2			
COMPASSES OF HISTORICAL HARPSICHORDS			
CC – f^3	FF – c^3	GG – c^3	C – e^2
EE – f^3	FF – b^2	GG – b^2	C – d^3
FF – a^3	FF – a^2	AA – f^3	C – c^3
FF – g^3	GG – g^3	AA – d^3	D – e^3
FF – f^3	GG – f^3	C – g^3	D – c^3
FF – e^3	GG – d^3	C – f^3	A – f^3

The String Scale. The matter of string scaling for the harpsichord refers to the length of the strings used in the instrument. It is customary simply to give the length of the string used for c^2 (Pitch C), since the length of the other strings in the instrument can be calculated easily from this one. Thus, for a specific harpsichord, the string scaling might be indicated as: c^2 = 12 inches.

As with the compass of the instrument, the scaling of the harpsichord, historically, has varied considerably. In the survey cited earlier, c^2 was found to range from 9 3/4 inches to 16 1/2 inches with an average length of 13 1/4 inches. Choosing the appropriate string scale depends upon the quality and quantity of sound one desires from the instrument. As the string scale is lengthened, the volume of sound increases since the mass of the string also increases. Obviously, the opposite also is true—shortening the string scale decreases the volume of sound available. Also, increasing the length of the string scale decreases the number of harmonics produced, thus tonal color is lost as volume is gained. However, excessive shortening of the string scale can lead to the point where the harmonics produced overpower the fundamental tone, so that the sound is generally confused.

The selection of a string scale for a specific harpsichord will depend upon the way the instrument will be used. If it is to be used in ensemble work, then extra color (more harmonics) is desirable so that it will stand out from the other instruments. This requires a shorter string scale. However, if the instrument is to be used as a solo concert instrument, then greater volume is desirable. This requires a longer string scale. In the final analysis, the string scale chosen usually is a compromise that will enable the instrument to sound best in the particular context for which it was designed but also to sound reasonably good in other contexts.

The lengthening of the string scale usually results in an increased tension on the instrument, so that the structure of the harpsichord may have to be substantially strengthened to withstand the pull of the strings. The increase in tension with an increase in the string scale comes about because, although theoretically it is possible to have a long string and a short string vibrate at the same frequency under the same tension, in musical instrument design this does not work. It does not work for the simple reason, as noted earlier, that the strings of a musical instrument sound best when under a tension that is close to the breaking point. Substituting a longer string for a shorter string under the same tension means using a string of a smaller diameter in order to maintain the same mass, and since strings of smaller diameter have lower breaking points, the result would be a broken string. Thus, in practice, as the string scale increases, so does the string size and tension. The appropriate gauge of wire to use for a specific string scale can be determined experimentally (see Table 1, which gives the tension and breaking point for various gauges of steel and brass music wire).

The final choice of a string scale for a particular instrument is a choice between tonal quality (shorter scales), sound quantity (longer scales), and greater tension (longer scales). It is possible to build an instrument with an extremely long scale, heavy strings, and high string tension. One even could build a steel frame into the instrument, like the plate in the piano, to withstand the pull of the strings. The resulting instrument, however, would tend to sound like a "plucked piano." Therefore, common sense dictates that the best-sounding harpsichord will be one with a string scale between 10 and 15 inches, with 12 inches probably being the optimum choice for a multi-function instrument.

The Number of Choirs. Besides selecting a string scale, the harpsichord designer also must determine the number of choirs, or sets of strings the instrument will have. The different choirs of strings are identified by terms borrowed from organ construction. Thus there are two-foot choirs, four-foot choirs, eight-foot choirs, and sixteen-foot choirs. The eight-foot choir is the standard set of strings on the harpsichord and it is tuned to normal pitch, so that the string representing c^1 (Middle C) vibrates at 216.15 cps, the same as c^1 on the piano. The term "eight-foot" is derived from the organ, wherein the pipe representing CC is eight feet long. In the sixteen-foot choir, the set of strings sound an octave lower than those of the eight-foot choir. The four-foot choir sounds an octave higher and the two-foot choir sounds two octaves higher than the eight-foot choir.

Most harpsichords have two eight-foot choirs, also known as unisons, which are indicated by this symbol: $2 \times 8'$. If, in addition to the unisons, there also is one four-foot choir (known as the octave), the three sets of strings would be indicated like this: $2 \times 8'$, $1 \times 4'$. There are eight different combinations of strings found on harpsichords with one, two, and, very rarely, three keyboards:

Single Keyboard
$1 \times 8'$
$2 \times 8'$
$1 \times 8'$, $1 \times 4'$
Double and Triple Keyboards
$2 \times 8'$, $1 \times 4'$
$1 \times 8'$, $1 \times 4'$
$1 \times 16'$, $1 \times 8'$, $1 \times 4'$
$1 \times 16'$, $2 \times 8'$, $1 \times 4'$
$1 \times 16'$, $2 \times 8'$, $1 \times 4'$, $1 \times 2'$

In choosing the number and kinds of choirs to be used in a harpsichord, one must remember that the greater number of choirs, the greater the range of expressiveness. This is gained, however, only at the expense of greater complexity and increased maintenance. The fewer the choirs, the less choice of expressiveness and the easier it is to keep the instrument tuned and regulated. Consequently, the

choice of the numbers and kinds of choirs a harpsichord will have depends on how the instrument is intended to be used. Practice instruments, as well as instruments for the amateur, should be kept as simple as possible. Concert instruments, on the other hand, can benefit from the greater expressiveness available from the more complex harpsichords.

The String Spacing. The string spacing is the distance between the strings of each choir in relation to one another and also in relation to other choirs. There are two dimensions involved in the spacing of the strings—vertical and horizontal. The vertical spacing is controlled by the number of different choirs of strings. The horizontal spacing is controlled by the octave span, or the spacing of the keys. The octave span of the keyboard is the distance measured between one edge of a natural key, such as C, to the same edge of the same key an octave higher, c, or lower, CC. The octave spans of harpsichords vary from 6 to 6 1/2 inches, with 6 1/4 inches being most common. Since there are 12 keys in an octave, this means that there only is about 1/2 inches allotted to each key at its tail end and, consequently, all of the strings for that key must be kept within that space. To complicate matters further, all of the jacks must also share that 1/2-inch space. The practical result is that, for the eight-foot choir, where a pair of unisons are almost universal, 3/8 inch of space is allocated to the jack. This is both to account for the jack's thickness and to provide room for it to move from the plucking position to the non-plucking, or off, position. This leaves a 1/8-inch space for the two strings in the unison. They are placed one to each side of the jack as shown in Figure 4.

When present, the sixteen-foot choir is located above the eight-foot, and the four-foot is located below the eight-foot choir. If there is a two-foot choir, it is located below the four-foot choir. The vertical and horizontal spacing of the strings must be arranged so that the vibrating strings do not strike against one another, a distinct possibility in the bass section. The spacing of the strings also must be arranged so that the plectra of the jacks for one choir do not accidentally pluck the strings of the choir above it. This arrangement is shown in Figure 4, where the vertical spacing is sufficient to prevent the strings from hitting one another and the horizontal offset of the strings prevents accidental plucking.

Calculating String Lengths. It is a well-known fact that a stretched string of a given size and tension will sound an octave lower if its length is doubled and an octave higher if its length is halved. Therefore, if the string scale for c^2 is 12 inches, then c^3 (an octave higher) will be 6 inches, and c^1 (an octave lower) will be 24 inches. With such a scale, one can continue the calculations and find that C would be 48 inches and CC 96 inches. However, this simple formula does not tell how to calculate the string lengths for all of the notes between the various Cs. An aid in determining the appropriate string lengths was developed by Marin Mersenne (1588–1648), a French mathematician. Table 3 shows the multipliers by which the length of the strings for any note within an octave can be determined, as long as the length of one of the strings is known. The first set of multipliers is for ascending the octave from a lower note to a higher note. The second set of multipliers is for descending the octave.

4. *String Spacing*

A. Eight-foot Jacks
B. Four-foot Jacks
C. Eight-foot Strings
D. Four-foot Strings
E. Jack Slides
F. Jack Guide
G. Keys

TABLE 3	
MERSENNE'S MULTIPLIERS	
Ascending	Descending
1.000	1.000
.944	1.060
.891	1.122
.841	1.190
.794	1.260
.749	1.334
.707	1.414
.667	1.498
.630	1.588
.595	1.682
.561	1.782
.530	1.888
.500	2.000

To use these multipliers, simply multiply the known string length, for example c² = 12 inches, by each of the multipliers:

$$12 \times 1.000 = 12.000 = c^2$$
$$12 \times .944 = 11.328 = c^{\#2}$$
$$12 \times .891 = 10.692 = d^2$$
$$12 \times .841 = 10.092 = d^{\#2}$$
etc.

or

$$12 \times 1.000 = 12.000 = c^2$$
$$12 \times 1.060 = 12.720 = b^1$$
$$12 \times 1.122 = 13.464 = b^{b1}$$
$$12 \times 1.190 = 14.280 = a^1$$
etc.

A simpler method if one has an electronic calculator is to multiply the known string length by the constant .94388, and then multiply the resultant product by the same number over and over again for the desired number of times as follows:

$$12.000 \times .94388 = 11.327 = c^{\#2}$$
$$11.327 \times .94388 = 10.691 = d^2$$
$$10.691 \times .94388 = 10.091 = d^{\#2}$$
$$10.091 \times .94388 = 9.525 = e^2$$
etc.

There are obvious differences in string lengths determined by the two methods of computation. These differences are not so significant as to alter greatly the sound or tension of an instrument. Of the two, the multiplier .94388 is the more accurate.

Using one of these two methods of calculation, one determines the different string lengths for a given octave and then multiplies each length by two for the next lower octave or divides by two for the next higher octave. One discovers, somewhat as a surprise, that by the time one reaches the note FF using c² = 12 inches, the length of the string is 143.808 inches, practically 12 feet! And, if instead of the eight-foot choir, a sixteen-foot choir were used, the same string would measure nearly 24 feet in length. For reasons cited earlier, strings of such great length are impractical in a harpsichord. As a result, a decision must be made as to the ac-

tual length the bass strings will be. This process is called foreshortening.

The amount of foreshortening that is to be used generally is determined by the overall size of the instrument. This means that the longest bass string is found by taking the overall intended length of the instrument and subtracting from that length the space taken up by the keys, the nameboard, the wrest plank in front of the nut, the soundboard between the bridge and the tail, and the thickness of the case at the tail. These measurements normally total from 12 to 16 inches in a single-manual harpsichord (an instrument with one keyboard) and considerably more in a double-manual (two keyboards) instrument. In the same survey cited earlier, the longest single-manual harpsichord was found to be 91 inches and the shortest 60 inches, with an average overall length of 78 inches; the longest double-manual harpsichord was 111 inches and the shortest 63 inches, with an overall average length of 93 inches. Unfortunately, due to the paucity of data available in the study, it was not possible to determine the actual length of the longest bass string for these particular instruments. However, from the data provided for certain other harpsichords, the longest bass string was 84 inches for a sixteen-foot GGG. The shortest bass string was 53 inches for an eight-foot C.

It was noted earlier that one of the desired characteristics for a harpsichord is the maintenance of an equal tension on all of the strings of the instrument. This means that, when a string is foreshortened from its theoretical length, its diameter must be increased in order to achieve the same mass as the longer string. While the wire size of a foreshortened string can be determined through trial and error simply by using the gauge of wire that sounds best, a more accurate means is through mathematical computation. For example, if the theoretical length of a string for a given note is 104 inches, and the proper wire size is .014 inch in diameter, and the foreshortened string for the same note has a length of 72 inches, then one squares the diameter of the wire, multiplies the square by the theoretical length, divides the product by the foreshortened length, and takes the square root of this sum. The resulting figure will be the diameter of the string necessary to achieve the same mass and, hence, the same frequency with the same tension:

$$(.014)^2 = .000196$$
$$.000196 \times 104 = .020384$$
$$.020384 \div 72 = .000283$$
$$\sqrt{.000283} = .016826$$

The wire gauge closest to .016826 inch is #6 with a diameter of .016 inch. This is the size of wire that should be used.

There are occasions when strings must be lengthened beyond their theoretical length in the treble section of the harpsichord. Usually this is necessary to provide sufficient space for the various ranks of jacks, especially in two-manual instruments with a four-foot choir. The process of determining the proper gauge for a stretched scale is the same as for the foreshortened scale.

Developing a String List. As the name implies, a string list is a table showing the lengths and wire gauges for all of the strings in a harpsichord. A typical string list for an eight-foot choir for a harpsichord is given in Table 4. It should be noted that in this string list the wire sizes begin to deviate from the theoretical at $f^{\#1}$. This does not mean that the strings are starting to be foreshortened at this point but, rather, that from an empirical point of view a heavier string sounds better than a lighter string beginning at this particular note. Piano manufacturers have recognized this phenomenon for a long time

and routinely change the gauge of their strings at every octave. Thus, if c^2 uses a #1 gauge wire, c^1 would use a #2, C a #3, etc.

The computation of the string lengths for a choir of strings in which the string sizes change by the octave requires a different set of multipliers than those given earlier. These multipliers are 1.89 for the octave and 1.0544 for the semitones. Given a string scale of $c^2 = 12$ inches, the computations would be as follows:

Octaves
$$12.00 \times 1.89 = 22.68 = c^1$$
$$22.68 \times 1.89 = 42.87 = c$$
$$42.87 \times 1.89 = 81.02 = C$$
etc.
Semitones
$$12.00 \times 1.0544 = 12.65 = b^1$$
$$12.65 \times 1.0544 = 13.34 = b^{b1}$$
$$13.34 \times 1.0544 = 14.07 = a^1$$
etc.

To extend the string list up the scale, simply divide rather than multiply by 1.89 for the octaves and 1.0544 for the semitones.

TABLE 4

A Typical String List*

Note	Wire size (in inches)	Wire gauge
$f^{\#1}$–c^1	.009	#0 steel
$f^{\#1}$–c^1	.010	1 steel
b – a	.011	2 steel
$g^{\#}$ – $f^{\#}$	.012	3 steel
f – $G^{\#}$	.014	5 steel
G – $D^{\#}$	.014	5 brass
D – C	.016	6 brass
BB – $AA^{\#}$	.018	7 brass
AA – $GG^{\#}$	.020	8 brass
GG – FF	.022	9 brass

* From Frank Hubbard's *Harpsichord Regulating and Repairing,* page 6. Tuners Supply, Inc., Boston, 1967.

The Keyboard

The function of the keys of the harpsichord is to transmit motion from the player's fingers to the jacks, causing the jacks to pluck the strings. The harpsichord keyboard consists of a series of individual keys representing naturals and accidentals in the same arrangement as the piano or organ. Each individual key is cut from wood and is pivoted near its midpoint on the balance pin, so when the key is pressed down by the player, the tail of the key rises, moving the jack up through the guides so that it can pluck the strings. A cross-sectional view of a keyboard is shown in Figure 3.

The balance rail pin (Figure 5) on which the key pivots is fixed in a hole in the balance rail. The balance rail is part of the key frame, which also has a back rail and a front rail as well as cross members that hold the various rails in their proper relationship to one another. When the key is at rest, it lies on the balance rail and the back rail. The front rail holds the front rail pins (Figure 5), which, in conjunction with the balance rail pins, serve to guide the key in its travel. The back rail is covered with a thick pad of felt to soften and silence the falling tail end of the key when it is released. This pad of felt is called a back rail cloth (Figure 6) and comes in various thicknesses to fit different keyboard designs. A small felt washer (Figure 6), called a balance rail pin punching, serves to silence the moving of the key around its pivot point and, in conjunction with paper punchings of various thicknesses, to level the keys on the key bed so that they present a uniform playing surface.

Front rail pin punchings of felt (Figure 6) are placed on the front rail pins between the keys and the front rail. The front rail punching is used to silence the descent of the front end of the key and also to limit the key dip, that is, the distance the key moves downward when it is depressed. The key dip can be adjusted to the proper amount by using different thicknesses of paper punchings under the felt punchings.

Both the balance rail pins and the front rail pins ride in mortises cut into the keys. Sometimes the mortises are bushed (lined) with a thin layer of felt called key bushing cloth; at other times the mortises are left unbushed and the pins rub directly against the wooden sides of the mortises. Though lighter, unbushed mortises are more difficult to form accurately, they are preferred since they offer the least amount of friction.

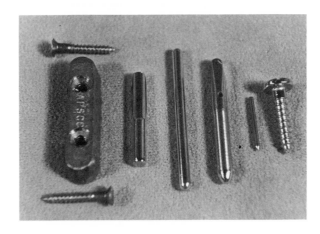

5. Harpsichord Hardware
Left to right: Jiffy Key Lead and Screws, Front Rail Pin, Balance Rail Pin, Tuning Pin, Center Pin, Flange Screw

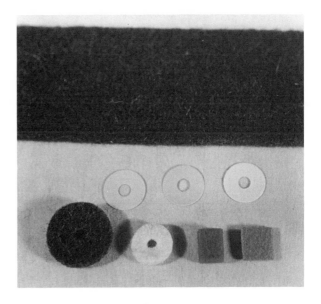

6. Harpsichord Felts
Top: Key and Jack Rail Cloth
Center: Paper Balance Rail Punchings
Bottom, left to right: Front Rail Punching, Balance Rail Punching, Harp Felt, Damper Cloth

Some harpsichords do not have a front rail pin, but, rather are fitted with a guide pin located near the tail of the key lever. This key guidance system works as well as the more conventional method described above. In addition, it has the advantage of being simpler to construct and adjust. This alternate method of key guidance is illustrated in Figure 7.

The octave span of the keys—that is, the distance measured between the same edge of two keys an octave apart—may vary from 6 to 6 1/2 inches. There seems to be little advantage of one span over the other. The narrower, 6 1/4-inch octave span presents an elegant appearance and seems to be the choice of most harpsichord builders over the 6 1/2-inch span of the piano. The length of the playing surface of the natural keys of the harpsichord—averaging around 5 inches in overall length—is somewhat shorter than that of the piano. The comb or raised portion of

the accidental key also is shorter, 3 inches being an average length. Otherwise the accidental key is the same size as that of the piano; it is 1/2 inch high and 1/2 inch wide, with tapered front and sides. Because there is a total of twelve keys in an octave, the tail end of each key in a keyboard with a 6 1/4-inch octave span will measure .521 inch minus the thickness of a saw cut, or about 1/2 inch wide.

The wooden body of the key is approximately 3/4 inch thick and is made from a light, straight-grained wood, free from knots. Among the more common woods used for the key bodies are clear white pine and basswood. The traditional white natural and black accidental pattern of the piano frequently is reversed on the harpsichord. As a consequence, a variety of materials are used for key coverings and for the combs of the accidentals. Materials commonly used for covering the natural keys are ebony, rosewood, or box-

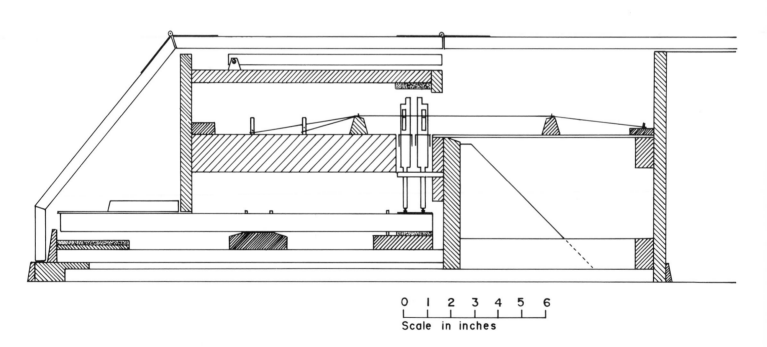

0 1 2 3 4 5 6
Scale in inches

7. Cross Section of Slant-cheeked Harpsichord

wood veneers, ivory, or the plastic ivory substitute known as Ivorine. Materials for the combs of the accidentals are selected to contrast well with the covering of the natural keys. These materials include rosewood, boxwood, holly, and ebony. The key fronts may be covered either with the same material used to cover the natural keys or with a contrasting material. Sometimes the key fronts have a molded cross section or are arcaded—a series of semi-circular moldings cut into the key fronts so that the row of keys gives the appearance of a series of arches or an arcade. See Figure 8.

The key frame usually is constructed from a strong, stable hardwood, such as maple, oak, or walnut. On occasion, the key frame is constructed from plywood to which the three rails are glued. If end pieces are a part of the key frame, they are made from the same material and finished in the same way as the case of the instrument.

Some criteria for a well-designed keyboard are:
1. The keys must work smoothly, noiselessly, and with a minimum of friction.
2. The keys should be long enough and the balance rail so located to avoid an awkward angle to the player when the keys are depressed.
3. The keys should be lightly weighted so a minimum of effort is required to play, yet sufficiently loaded so they can return promptly to the rest position when released.
4. The playing surface of the keys should be level and even from one key to the next.
5. The key dip should measure between 5/16 and 3/8 inch.
6. The materials used to cover the natural keys and the combs of the accidentals should be selected to present a harmonious appearance and to be durable enough to withstand hard usage.

8. Molded Key Fronts

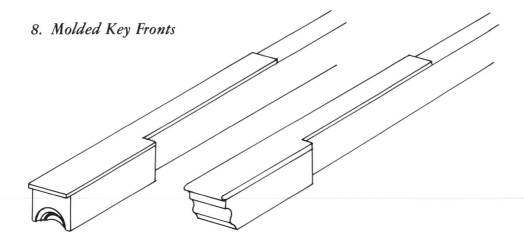

The Jacks

The jack of the harpsichord is responsible for the actual plucking of the string. A typical jack is illustrated in Figure 9 and consists of the following parts: jack body, tongue, axle pin, jack spring, plectrum, tongue adjusting screw, and damper. The jack operates in the following manner:

The jack rests on the end of a key, its height such that the plectrum lies just under the string it is to pluck. As the key is depressed, the jack rises, the damper is lifted off the string, and the plectrum is forced past the string, therefore plucking it. As long as the key is depressed, the string will continue to vibrate, since, in this position, the damper and plectrum are above the string. When the key is released, the jack descends. During this descent, as the plectrum touches the string, rather than plucking again, it slides around the string by means of the pivoting tongue; that is, the tongue pivots backward on its axle until the plectrum is able to clear the string. This backward motion is facilitated by the bevel cut on the underside of the plectrum at its tip. Once the plectrum reaches a position beneath the string, the tongue is returned to the normal plucking position by the jack spring. Also, at the same time that the plectrum is passing the string on its descent, the damper comes to rest on the string, silencing its vibrations.

With the exception of the lute jack, which shares the same string with one of the eight-foot jacks, there is a jack for every string. Thus a harpsichord with a range of FF to f³ and two eight-foot choirs of strings would have 61 strings and 61 jacks for each choir, or a total of 122 jacks.

Generally, each jack rests on a single key, so in a two-manual instrument, one of the keyboards controls certain ranks of jacks and the other keyboard the other ranks of jacks. One exception is the dogleg jack (Figure 10), which is so designed that it rests on both keyboards simultaneously. The dogleg jack was designed to be played from either keyboard. In most contemporary instruments, its function has been taken over by the keyboard coupler.

Jack bodies vary considerably in size, ranging from 3/8 to 5/8 inch or more in width, 1/8 to 3/16 inch in thickness, and 4 to 6 inches or more in length. The actual size of the jack body depends upon the layout of the instrument and the size of the slots in the jack guides, since it is easier to cut a jack to fit a specific size slot than the reverse.

The jack body needs to be constructed from a material that possesses strength, smoothness of surface, and a low coefficient of sound transmission so it will operate noiselessly in its slot. Wood and plastic are among the more common materials used for jack bodies. Some of the woods employed are pearwood, walnut, maple, beech, and mahogany. In fact, almost any straight-grained hardwood capable of taking a high polish can be used for jack bodies. Among the plastics used in the construction of jack bodies are Delrin, nylon, Plexiglas, and hard rubber. Plastic bodies are preferable to wood ones, since they do not swell and shrink with changes in humidity as much as wood does. Wooden jack bodies, especially when used with wooden jack guides, tend to stick in the summer and rattle in the winter as a consequence of changing humidity. This, of course, leads to difficulties in keeping the harpsichord properly regulated.

The tongue of the jack generally is of the same material as the jack body. It normally is about 1″ × 1/8″ × 3/16″ in size. The top of the tongue is cut at an angle, so the adjusting screw can cause it to move back as the screw is advanced. The tongue has a square hole in it about 3/32″ × 3/32″ when leather is used for a plectrum and since plastic is stiffer, a rectangular hole about 1/50″ × 3/32″ when it is used for the plectrum. On the rear side of the tongue there is a small

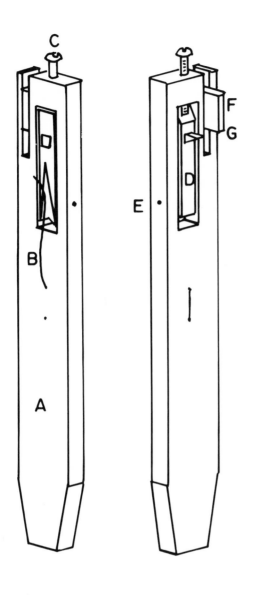

9. A Typical Jack

A. Jack Body   E. Axle Pin
B. Jack Spring   F. Damper
C. Tongue-adjusting Screw   G. Plectrum
D. Tongue

10. A Dogleg Jack

"V" groove, whose purpose is to keep the jack spring in place.

Leather and plastic are the two materials in general use for the plectra of harpsichords. If the plectrum is of leather, it is made of sole leather and is shaped, during voicing, as shown in Figure 11. The top of the plectrum is the tanned surface of the leather. If the plectrum is made of plastic, Delrin is the material most often used, and it is shaped during voicing as shown in Figure 11.

The jack spring usually is made of brass music wire .010 or .011 inch in diameter. On occasion a nylon monofilament of a somewhat larger diameter is used. The spring is fixed in a hole in the body of the jack, usually with an appropriate cement. The upper end of the spring where it contacts the groove in the tongue is bent slightly outward so that the end does not dig into the material of the tongue. The jack spring is illustrated in Figure 9.

The axle on which the tongue pivots generally is made from a length of brass spring wire about .031 inch in diameter. However, small-diameter center pins and even common straight pins have been used on occasion. Some commercial plastic tongues have the axles molded to them as integral parts. Such tongues merely snap into holes drilled in the jack bodies.

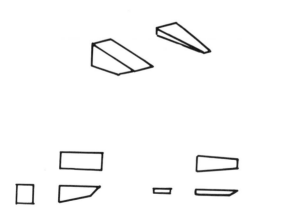

11. *Details of Plastic and Leather Plectra*

The tongue adjusting screw may be either a brass or steel round-head machine screw with a 2-56 thread from 1/2 to 3/4 inch in length, depending on the design of the jack. Sometimes a slotted, headless set-screw is used, so no part of the screw projects above the jack body. The threaded end pin usually is specially designed to ride in a hole drilled in the jack guide. In this way it can serve both to guide the bottom end of the jack as well as to adjust the effective length of the jack. Normally the end pin is made of brass with a body diameter of 1/8 to 3/16 inch, an overall length of from 1 1/4 to 1 3/4 inches, with a 4–40 thread on the threaded portion. A hole drilled through the end pin near its bottom end allows a small rod to be used to screw it in or out of the jack body.

The damper is used to silence the vibrations of the string when the jack is in a resting position. The damper must work with the jack slide in both the on and the off positions to silence any sympathetic vibrations even when the jack is not active. The damper usually is made of a small piece of felt wedged into a slot in the jack as shown in Figure 9. Sometimes the damper may be cemented to a brass clip, which can be adjusted to its proper position by sliding it up or down the jack body. The length of the damper must be adapted to the string spacing so it does not extend so far as to dampen a string in an adjoining course. Similarly, when eight-foot, four-foot, and sixteen-foot jacks are used in conjunction with one another, the width of the damper must be narrow enough not to touch the other strings when the jack is in play.

The Jack Slides. The jack is guided in its travel by the jack slide and the jack guide. The jack slide is a movable strip of wood, metal, or plastic fitted level with and in the gap between the wrest plank and the soundboard. The jack slide has slots cut into it to correspond to the shape and size of the jack body in cross-

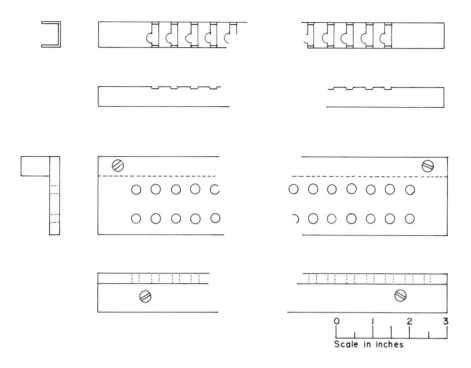

12. *Plan for Jack Slides and Guide*

13. *Slotting the Jack Slides*

section. The slots are spaced according to the string spacing of the harpsichord. A typical jack slide is illustrated in Figure 12.

In most instances the jack slide is made from a piece of brass or aluminum channel whose inside width is the same as the width of the jack body. The slots are produced by milling the channel crosswise with a metal slotting saw chosen so the slot cut by the blade will be the same as the thickness of the jack body. On occasion, the jack slide is made by punching rectangular slots through thin sheet metal or plastic and then mounting these sheets on small bars to achieve the necessary rigidity. Wooden slides are produced in a similar manner by simply forming the wood stock into a channel with a dado saw before cutting the crosswise slots.

The jack slides usually rest on the two blocks that project into the gap between the wrest plank and the belly rail. Sometimes, especially with jack slides that are flexible, additional support is provided by spacers, made either of wood or metal, which span the gap. These spacers also serve to brace the belly rail against the tension of the strings. When used, the spacers must be accurately positioned so that they will not interfere with the movement of the jacks in either the on or the off position.

The Jack Guide. The jack guide (Figure 12) works in conjunction with the jack slides to hold the jacks in correct alignment with the strings. The jack guide is mounted below the jack slides in a fixed position. It is attached just above the keys to either the belly rail or the wrest plank, or both. The jack guide is a strip of wood, metal, or plastic that either has slots cut in it to correspond to the shape of the jack body or has holes drilled in it to correspond to the diameter of the end pin in the jack or to the diagonal measurement of the thinned section of the jack body. In both cases, the spacing is identical to that of the jack slide.

The Jack Rail. Because the action of the jacks when being played can be rather lively, a jack rail (Figure 3) is fixed directly above the tops of the jacks to prevent them from jumping out of their slides. The jack rail runs across the width of the case. It is made of wood covered on the underside with felt. Some means is provided to easily remove the jack rail from the harpsichord so there is access to the jacks for adjustment purposes.

In some instruments the jack rail, in addition to keeping the jacks in their slides, also serves to determine the amount of key dip in the harpsichord. In these cases there is no front rail cloth or punchings in the key frame. The key is stopped in its downward motion by the top of the jack touching the bottom of the jack rail where it is covered with felt. When this method of controlling key dip is used, it is essential that the tops of all of the jacks project an equal distance above the strings. Normally, with such jacks headless, tongue-adjusting screws are used so they can be buried in the top of the jack bodies and, thus, not project unevenly above the jacks.

The Soundboard

The soundboard of the harpsichord serves to transmit sound waves from a vibrating string to the surrounding air. Because of its small surface area, a vibrating string suspended in air is a poor radiator of sound energy. In contrast, the soundboard of a harpsichord has a large surface area and can transmit effectively the sound energy of a vibrating string to the air. Even though the sound of a vibrating string transmitted through a soundboard will be louder than the sound of an unassisted string, it is erroneous to speak of the soundboard as an amplifier, since the soundboard does not contribute any energy to the sound waves. What happens is that the louder sound coming from the soundboard consumes energy from the string at a faster rate than the string does alone. Consequently, the louder sound from the soundboard will last for a shorter period of time than the weaker sound from the unassisted string.

The soundboard of the harpsichord usually is made from wood and averages about 1/8 inch in thickness. The most common wood used in contemporary instruments is quarter-sawed spruce. In quarter-sawed wood, the growth rings are vertical to the surface of the wood. This gives the wood physical qualities similar to corrugated cardboard, in that the wood is quite flexible across the grain and fairly stiff with the grain. This flexible quality leads to a rapid transmission of sound across the soundboard, while the stiffness of the length of the grain helps to brace the soundboard against the downward and twisting pressures exerted by the strings on the bridge.

Some harpsichord-makers use 1/8-inch basswood plywood for the soundboard as insurance against the soundboard cracking with changes in humidity. Other makers use specially treated sheet aluminum for the soundboard. However, since so many factors such as the strings, string scale, and plucking points, in addition to the soundboard, contribute to the quality of sound of a specific instrument, and since no empirical studies comparing one soundboard material to another have been conducted, it is not possible to prove the desirability of one material over another for soundboard construction.

The Soundboard Bracing. The harpsichord soundboard is braced on the underside with wooden ribs. The bridge on the upperside also serves as a brace. The bracing of the sound board is designed to withstand the pressure of the strings and to isolate the resonating area from the nonresonating area of the soundboard.

An unbraced soundboard will collapse under the downward pressure of the strings. More important, though, in an unbraced soundboard, sound vibrations travel across the entire surface and, in the process, some desirable harmonics are filtered out. It also results in less sound output, since an unbraced soundboard is a very inefficient transmitter of sound. Through the use of a series of braces, a portion of the soundboard can be prevented from vibrating and the energy of the strings can be concentrated in the unrestricted area. This leads to a greater output of sound and, if the position of the braces is carefully selected, some control over the filtering effect of the soundboard can be attained. In general, the smaller the unrestricted area of the soundboard the higher the range of frequencies that will be reinforced. Conversely, the larger the unrestricted area of the soundboard, the lower the range of frequencies that will be reinforced.

The traditional and most practical system of soundboard bracing is illustrated in Figure 14. The long bar parallel to the bridge is called the cutoff bar. It serves both to support the soundboard and, as noted above, to isolate the resonating portion from the nonresonating portion of the soundboard. As can be seen, there are no braces in the area of the bridge, since the bridge, because of its rigidity, serves to brace this portion of the soundboard. In addition to the cutoff bar, there are several smaller braces used to dampen vibrations and to support the non-vibrating area of the soundboard. These braces are placed perpendicular to the soundboard and at a right angle to the cutoff bar.

The second mode of bracing is called crossbarring (Figure 15). In crossbarring, a series of parallel braces are fastened to the soundboard at approximately right angles to and running directly under the bridge. Because there is a certain amount of dampening of vibrations where the braces cross under the bridge, some builders cut away the braces in the area next to the bridge providing, in effect, two sets of braces, one on each side of the bridge.

The braces used to reinforce the

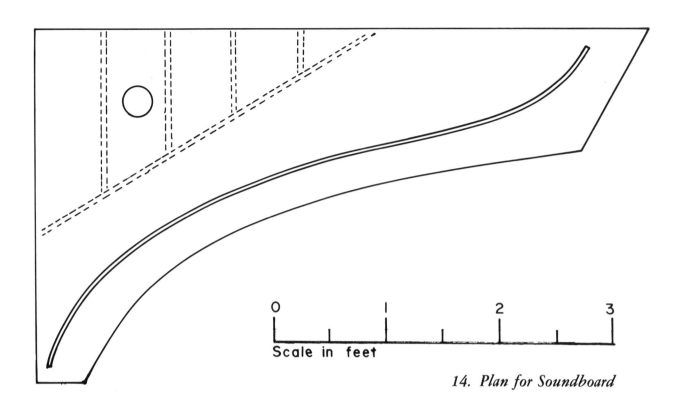

0   1   2   3

Scale in feet

14. Plan for Soundboard

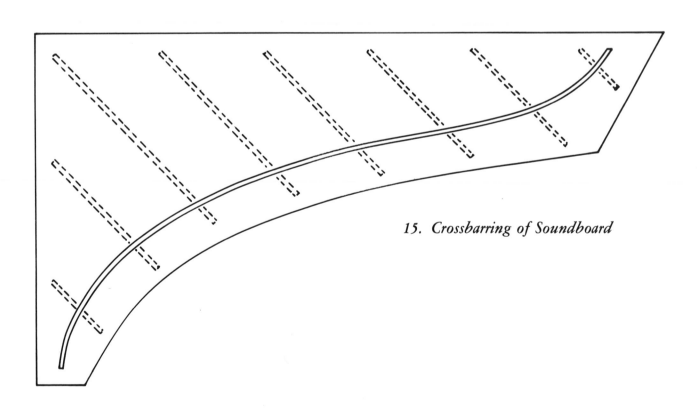

15. Crossbarring of Soundboard

soundboard usually are made of flat-sawed spruce so that the growth rings are perpendicular to the soundboard. The cutoff bar usually is 3/8 to 1/2 inch in thickness, 1 1/2 to 2 1/2 inches in height, with the length being determined by the design of the harpsichord. The smaller braces usually are 1/4 to 3/8 inch thick by 1 to 1 1/2 inches in height.

Most harpsichords have a sound hole in the soundboard. The sound hole is from 2 1/2 to 3 1/2 inches in diameter and may be ornamented in much the same fashion as the sound hole of the lute or simply left undecorated. There are harpsichords, however, that have no sound holes or other openings in the soundbox. Because of the lack of controlled experimentation, there is no scientific evidence in support of or against the presence of a sound hole. Since we do not know the effect of the sound hole on the quality of sound, the matter is left to the preference of the designer. It is recommended, however, that there be an opening somewhere in the sound box to provide for the equalization of air pressure.

Closely associated with the soundboard is the sound box. The sound box is a resonating cavity of air that helps to couple the vibration of the soundboard to the surrounding air. The sound box of the harpsichord consists of the volume of air enclosed between the soundboard and the bottom of the harpsichord case. It is bounded by the belly rail, spine, tail, bent side, and cheek of the case. Each of the parts enumerated contributes to the complex pattern of resonance of the sound box.

The soundboard–sound box configuration of the harpsichord probably contributes more to the final sound quality of the instrument than all the other parts put together. This being the case, there is surprisingly little information or hard scientific evidence on what particular soundboard–sound box configuration would produce what kinds of acoustical results. True, some builders con-tinually experiment with the design of the instrument, but rarely is this experimentation carried out in such a way as to allow for comparing the experimental instrument with a second instrument identical in all respects except for a specific modification. Lacking this control, judgments about the effect of the experiment turn out to be qualitative rather than quantitative. Until such a time as more scientific evidence is available, the designer must be guided by tradition, copying that which has worked well in the past and modifying only enough to meet contemporary musical needs.

The Bridge. While it is the primary function of the bridge to transmit the sound waves from the vibrating strings to the soundboard, there is some evidence that the bridge also acts as a filter, dampening certain vibrations while allowing others to pass through. A second function of the bridge is to act as a brace for the soundboard, strengthening the soundboard around and under it against the downward pressure exerted by the strings. A third function of the bridge is to receive the bridge pins, which control the spacing of the strings.

The bridge of the harpsichord is made from a dense hardwood, such as walnut, beech, or maple. It usually is sawed from a single piece of wood, although—especially in production models—it may be built up by lamination, in which thin layers of wood are bent and glued together in the desired shape. In cross-section the bridge is formed as shown in Figure 3. It should be noted that the top of the bridge slopes in both directions, so the very apex controls the height of the strings above the soundboard while the strings touch the bridge pins a short distance away from this apex and toward the wrest plank.

The bridge pins (Figure 5) are small, pointed metal rods about 1/16 inch in diameter and 1/2 to 3/4 inch in length. They are similar in appearance to small, headless nails. The bridge pins are driven into holes drilled in the bridge so that 1/8 inch or less projects above the top of the bridge. These pins serve two functions. The first is to control the spacing between the strings. The second is to provide a metal-to-metal cutoff point for the vibrating length of the string, as can be seen in Figure 16. Usually there is a single bridge pin for each string. However, some makers provide two bridge pins for each string. This is called double pinning. When double pinning is used, the string snakes its way between two bridge pins, as shown in Figure 17. Builders using this method claim that the bearing is more positive.

Normally, separate bridges and nuts are provided for the four-foot, eight-foot, and sixteen-foot choirs. When a four-foot choir (Figure 16) is present, its bridge will be lower than that of the eight-foot choir, ranging in height from 3/8 to 1/2 inch. The hitch-pin rail for the four-foot choir is fastened to the underside of the soundboard and spaced about halfway between the four-foot and the eight-foot bridges. The eight-foot bridge usually carries two unisons and ranges from 1/2 to 1 1/4 inches in height. When a four-foot choir also is present, the height of the eight-foot bridge must be about twice the height of the four-foot bridge to insure that the dampers on the four-foot jacks do not touch the strings of the eight-foot choir when in

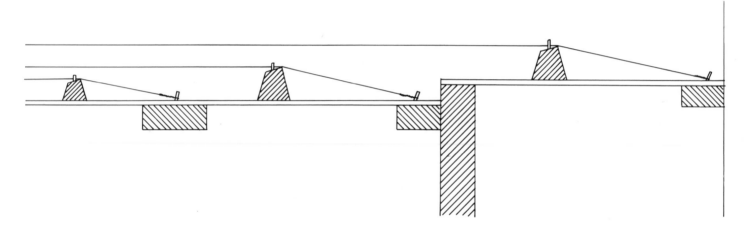

16. *Arrangement of Bridges and Hitch Pin Rails*

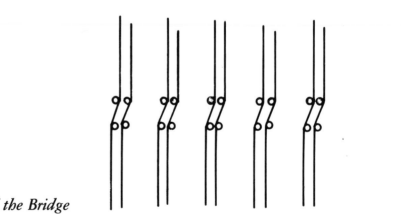

17. *Double Pinning of the Bridge*

play. Usually 3/8 to 1/2 inch is sufficient spacing for this purpose.

The sixteen-foot bridge (Figure 16) is higher than the eight-foot bridge. When a sixteen-foot bridge is used, it is customary to provide a separate hitch-pin rail for the eight-foot choirs by constructing a rail extending from the bottom of the case upward to the soundboard in the same place the eight-foot hitch-pin rail would be if there were no sixteen-foot choir. In effect, this hitch-pin rail divides the sixteen-foot soundboard from the remainder of the soundboard, thus providing a separate soundboard for the sixteen-foot bridge.

The Hitch-Pin Rail and Soundboard Molding.

At their extreme end, the strings of the harpsichord are attached to hitch pins embedded in the hitch-pin rail (Figure 16). The strings run from the hitch pins across the bridge on the soundboard, across the nut (a second bridge) on the wrest plank, and terminate at the tuning pins, which are embedded in the wrest plank.

Normally there is one hitch pin to a string in the harpsichord. The string is fastened to the hitch pin with a twisted loop similar to the one illustrated in Figure 18. However, some contemporary makers employ only one hitch pin for every two strings. When this is the case, the string simply passes around the hitch pin and is secured only to the tuning pins. Interestingly enough, when the two strings are tightened to a reasonable tension with this system, they act independently of one another, so the tuning of one string does not affect the tuning of the other.

18. Hitch Pin Loop

The pins used in the hitch-pin rail are the same as those used in the bridge. That is, both the bridge pins and the hitch pins are center pins such as those used in piano flanges. These center pins are available in a variety of sizes ranging from #18 (.046 inch in diameter) to #26 (.066 inch in diameter). The hitch pins are driven into small, pre-drilled holes in the hitch-pin rail so they protrude about 1/8 to 3/16 inch above the surface. The hitch pins are spaced so that the strings make an angle of approximately 15 degrees toward the treble side as they leave the bridge, and, since the hitch-pin rail is lower than the bridge, the strings also angle downward from the bridge to the hitch pin, as shown in Figure 16. The reason for this sideways and downward bearing of the strings is to insure that the strings rest firmly against the top of the bridge, which controls the height of the strings, and securely against the bridge pins, which control the spacing of the strings.

The Wrest Plank

The wrest plank in the harpsichord consists of a large piece of hardwood that reaches across the harpsichord from one side to the other. It is located just behind and above the playing surface of the keys; its top is level with the top of the soundboard as shown in Figure 3. The wrest plank has several functions: it holds the tuning pins; it supports the nut; and it is that part of the harpsichord to which the harp stop, jack-slide-regulating mechanism, and hand stops are attached.

Traditionally, the wrest plank is constructed from a solid block of clear, hard maple. It may range in thickness from 1 1/2 to 2 1/2 inches. Its width and length are determined by the design of the instrument. The greater the compass of the harpsichord, the longer the wrest plank; the more string choirs present, the more space needed for tuning pins and nuts, hence the wider the wrest plank. Some harpsichord makers prefer using a laminated wrest plank rather than one fashioned from a solid block of wood. They believe that a laminated plank holds the tuning pins more securely and thereby contributes to tuning stability. It is doubtful that such an elaborate wrest plank is needed in view of the modest tension it must withstand.

The wrest plank is joined to the harpsichord case by the wrest plank blocks. These blocks are constructed from a hardwood, such as maple, and are fastened to both the bottom and the sides of the harpsichord case. They are designed to provide a gap for the jack slides between the front edge of the wrest plank and the belly rail.

Some makers provide spacers between the front edge of the wrest plank and the belly rail to spread the tension on the instrument more evenly across its entire width and to help prevent the belly rail from bowing inward and binding the jack slides in the gap.

The Nut. The nut on the wrest plank (Figure 3) is a second bridge identical in material and cross-sectional shape to the soundboard bridge. The nut is not double-pinned, for this would impede the tuning of the instrument. It usually is straight throughout its length, though some harpsichord builders, in an effort to secure the optimum plucking point for the strings, use a nut that curves somewhat in the bass section. A four-foot nut, when present, will be lower and will be placed in front of the eight-foot nut on the wrest plank. The sixteen-foot nut, when present, will be higher and will be placed behind the eight-foot nut on the wrest plank.

The Tuning Pins. The final point of attachment for the strings of the harpsichord are the tuning pins (Figure 5), which are much smaller in diameter and shorter in length than those used in the piano. In fact, pins designed for use in the zither or the autoharp are the same as those used in most contemporary harpsichords. It is possible to use such small

tuning pins because the tension on the strings of a harpsichord is much less than that on the strings of a piano. For example, a string for a harpsichord at c^2 may be at a tension of 8 1/2 pounds, whereas a string at the same pitch on the piano may be at a tension of 175 pounds—a twenty-fold increase in tension. Because of this low tension, tuning problems encountered in the harpsichord seldom are a result of tuning-pin failure.

As the name suggests, the function of the tuning pin is to allow a particular string to be tuned to a specific frequency by increasing or decreasing its tension. The tuning pin is a type of wood screw—its upper end is square to fit the tuning wrench and has a hole in which the string is fastened; its lower end is round and shallowly threaded. The pitch of the thread is very small, so the tuning pin is pulled only a short distance into the wrest plank with each revolution of the pin. The typical tuning pin used in the harpsichord is .198 inch in diameter and 1 3/4 inches long. It is manufactured from steel and can be purchased with either a nickel-plate or a blue, rust-resistant finish.

The holes for the tuning pins are drilled in rows across the wrest plank directly behind the bridge they are to serve. A separate row of holes is provided for each choir of strings. Sometimes the holes for the tuning pins are drilled in a straight line, and sometimes they are staggered in a pattern that resembles the pattern of the keys, so the tuning pins for the sharps and flats are slightly in front of those for the naturals (Figure 19). Occasionally, because of space problems, the strings for the treble end of the four-foot choir may pass through holes in the eight-foot bridge to tuning pins that are located directly in front of the tuning pins for the eight-foot strings.

The Harp Stop. The harp stop, also known as the buff stop, (Figure 20) consists of a batten of wood that has small projections on which

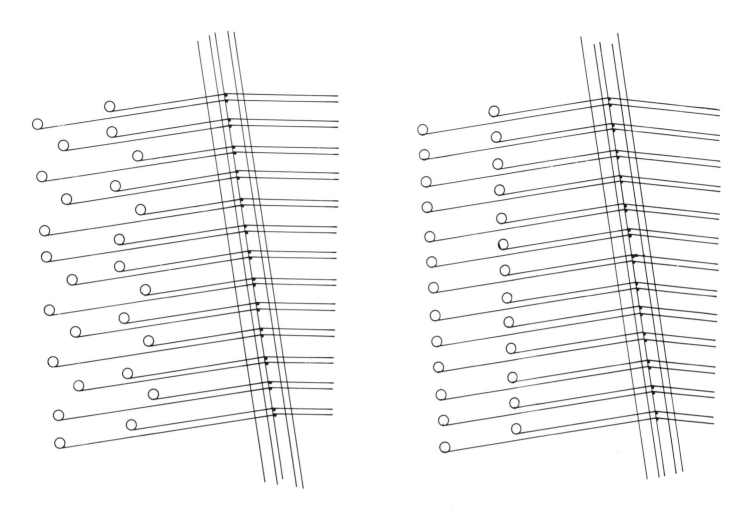

19. *Staggered and Conventional Tuning Pin Arrangement*

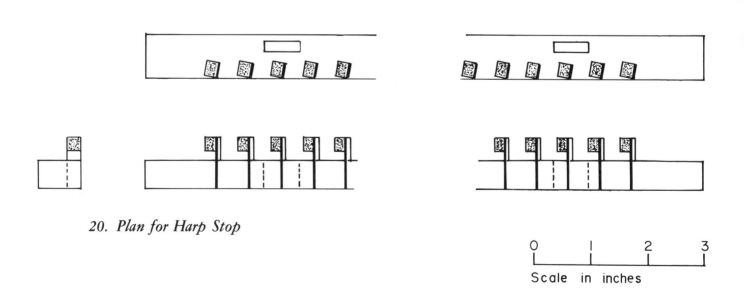

20. *Plan for Harp Stop*

Scale in inches

are glued small pads of buff leather felt, or other soft material. The harp stop is located right next to the nut and, when engaged, the small pads touch lightly upon each string in the choir, dampening and therefore eliminating many of the partials. The resultant sound is less metallic, soft, and harp-like.

The Stop Mechanism. The jack slides and harp stop must be equipped with some means for moving them from the off to the on position and vice versa. This enables the player to select a registration appropriate to the music being played. Because of the thickness of the jack and the spacing of the strings, less than 3/32 inch of motion in the jack slide is possible. This must be controlled accurately, especially in the on position, if the instrument is to operate properly.

The two most common mechanisms used to control the movement of the jack slide are the lever and the cam. The lever (Figure 21) is the least complex of the two mechanisms. In its simplest form, the lever consists of a bar of metal with one end linked to the jack slide. The opposite end of the lever is formed into a handle that projects through

a slot cut into the nameboard in the area directly above the keyboard. The bar is pivoted at a point close to its connection to the jack slide, so as the handle moves through 1/2-inch or more of travel, the jack slide at the opposite end of the bar will move through 1/8-inch or less of travel. The precise on and off position of the jack slide in such an arrangement usually is controlled by capstan screws fastened to the case at each end of the jack slide. By turning these screws in or out, the setting for the on position and the distance to the off position can be controlled precisely.

The lever control mechanism is adequate for an instrument with only two registers. When more than two registers are required in the harpsichord, the simple lever mechanism no longer will function satisfactorily due to restrictions of space and the need to maintain equal lever action on all stops. More complicated systems utilizing cams to control the movement of the jack slides have been developed to surmount these problems. One such cam system is illustrated in Figure 22. (It should be noted that this particular mechanism is protected by patent and,

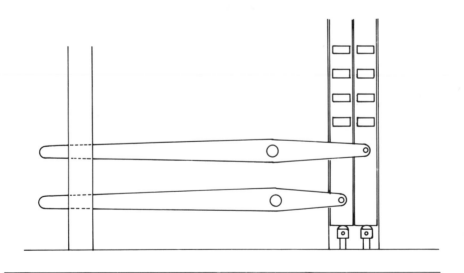

21. *Lever Hand Stop*

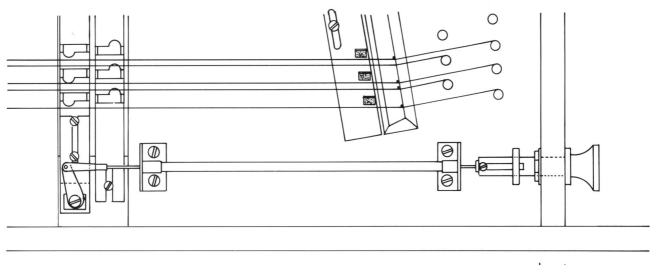

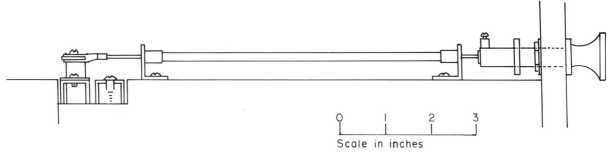

Scale in inches

22. Plan for Hand Stop for Back Eight Foot Jack Slide

23. View of Hand Stop for Back Eight Foot Jack Slide

therefore, cannot be manufactured for commercial purposes without the express permission of the inventor. For more information contact the publisher of this book.)

In this system the cam consists of an eccentric cylinder that rotates on an axle fastened to the wrest plank block. The cam has a short lever projecting from its upper end. When this lever moves through a turn of 90 degrees, about 3/4 inch at the end, the eccentricity of the cam causes a sideways motion of about 3/32 inch. The cam follower consists of a piece of sheet metal that is pierced with a rectangular hole, its width precisely the diameter of the cam. The follower is attached

to the jack slide with bolts passing through a slot in the follower. This slot allows for the precise adjustment of the off and on position of the jack slide. The cam lever is attached, by a cable enclosed in a housing, to the hand stop or pedal mechanism of the instrument. By lengthening the barrel of the cam, the position of the cam levers can be stacked one above the other to accommodate the necessary number of mechanisms in the small space alloted to them.

Note that in any linkage system a certain amount of slack or play is bound to develop. Usually this play is most noticeable in the push rather than the pull position. This

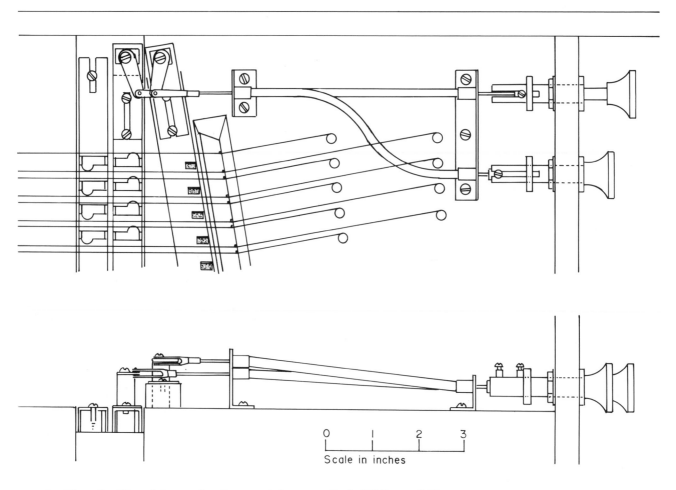

24. Plan for Hand Stops for Front Eight Foot Jack Slide and Harp

25. View of Hand Stops for Front Eight Foot Jack Slide and Harp

being the case, the pull position should be the on position for the jack slide, since this is the most critical setting.

In some harpsichords a pedal is used instead of a hand stop to control the movement of the jack slide. The harpsichord pedal (Figure 26) is a simple lever that can move sideways as well as up and down. The pedal is spring loaded so it will return automatically to the off or up position when released. When the pedal is depressed it can be moved sideways by the foot into a notch that locks it in the on position. This locking action permits the pedal to remain in the on position when the player's foot is removed from the pedal. A slight sideways pressure in the opposite direction removes the pedal from the locked position and allows it to return to the off position. Obviously, the bearings of the harpsichord pedal have to be constructed to allow this two-way action.

The harpsichord pedal usually is connected to the jack slide mechanism by a series of rods and levers. To take up excessive play in the pedal linkage that may develop through wear, the pedal rod, which connects the movement of the pedal to the mechanism in or under the harpsichord case, usually is capable of being shortened or lengthened by a simple screw action.

Some mention must be made of the keyboard coupler in this discussion of the stop mechanism. As the name suggests, the keyboard coupler is used in two-manual harpsichords to couple or connect the upper keyboard to the lower keyboard. This allows the jacks assigned to the upper keyboard to be played from the lower keyboard. The least complex form of keyboard coupler is known as the shove coupler (Figure 27). There are various different types of shove couplers, but all work on the same principle—a movable upper keyboard is fixed on slides so it can be shoved in a short distance to engage the coupling mechanism or pulled out a similar distance to disengage the coupling mechanism. In the simplest shove coupler, there is an upright wooden projection fastened to the tails of the keys in the lower manual. When the upper keyboard is shoved in, these projections just touch the bottom of the upper keys. Thus, when a lower key is depressed at its playing end, the projection pushes up on the tail of a matching key in the upper keyboard,

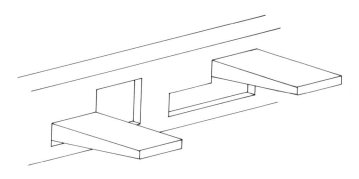

26. *Pedal Lock*

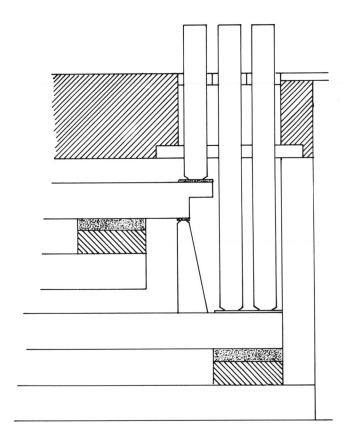

27. *Keyboard Coupler*

42

causing any jacks assigned to that key to play, providing their slides are in the on position. When the upper keyboard is pulled out to disengage the coupler, the projections on the lower keys are lined up with notches cut in the underside of the keys on the upper keyboard. Thus, when the lower keyboard is played, the projections on the keys move into the notches and the upper keyboard acts independently of the lower keyboard.

The Harpsichord Case

The harpsichord case surrounds and contains the various working parts of the instrument. The case provides structural strength to withstand the tension of the strings and serves to maintain the various parts of the instrument, such as the keyboard, jacks, and strings in the proper relationship to one another. The case also protects the internal workings of the instrument from accidental damage, functions as a working part of the sound box, and presents the viewer with an aesthetic object to behold.

The harpsichord case (Figure 2) has five sides: the long side or spine, the tail, the curved side commonly called the bent side, and the short side or cheek. The fifth side of the instrument is the opening in which the keyboard is located. In addition to the sides of the case, there are also a bottom, a belly rail, and various braces and other rails.

The sides and bottom of most modern harpsichords are constructed from 1/2 or 3/4 inch hardwood plywood. The various rails and braces are made from either softwood or hardwood lumber depending upon the specific function each is to serve. With the exception of the bent side, the construction of the harpsichord case follows conventional cabinet-making practices. The bent side must be glued up from thin laminae, or layers, of wood; the curvature is controlled by a special jig that holds the laminae in place until the glue sets.

The harpsichord case generally is veneered with hardwood. Moldings and other visible wooden parts are constructed of solid hardwood of the same variety of wood as the veneer. The finish used on the case may be boiled linseed oil, varnish, or any one of the numerous wood-finishing products on the market. Some harpsichord-makers choose to paint the case of the instrument. This especially is the case if they are making a replica of an historic instrument.

The Case Bracing. The most important aspect of the harpsichord case is the size and arrangement of the bracing inside the sound-box cavity. These braces serve to withstand the stresses imposed on the instrument by the stretched strings. This tension is unequally spread over the length of the case. The greatest tension is concentrated in the treble end of the instrument, where the bridge curve is the greatest; the least tension is along the relatively straight portion of the bent side. Because of this uneven tension, there is a tendency for the case of the instrument to curve or pull upward from the treble bent side end to the tail of the harpsichord; this curve is similar to the curl found in an airplane propeller. There also is a tendency for the case to collapse onto the wrest plank from this same string tension. Consequently, the design and placement of the braces are critical to the success of the instrument.

A practical system for bracing the case of the harpsichord consists of a series of triangular braces fitted between the belly rail and the bottom of the case. A second series of braces run diagonally from the bent side forward to either the belly rail or the spine, depending upon the location of the specific brace. These braces are fastened not only to the bent side and the belly rail or spine, but also to the bottom of the harpsichord case. Figure 28 illustrates this system of bracing. Figure 30 shows the shape of a typical bent side brace.

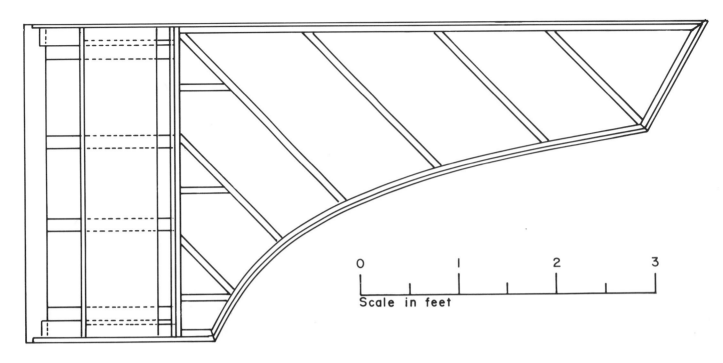

28. *Plan for Case*

29. *Interior of Case*

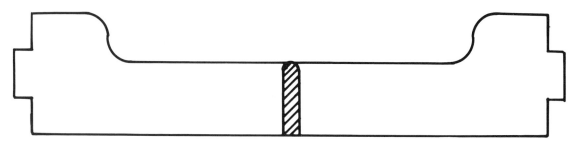

30. *Typical Sound Box Brace*

31. *Interior of Sound Box*

The Nameboard. The nameboard (Figures 3 and 7) of the harpsichord is a piece of trim on which the name of the builder is frequently found. Its major function, however, is to close the gap between the keyboard and the wrest plank. The nameboard is fitted so that there is about 1/8 inch of clearance between its bottom edge and the top surface of the key levers. There also should be 1/8-inch clearance between the front of the nameboard and the ends of the combs of the accidental keys.

The Music Desk. Although not essential to the operation of the harpsichord, the music desk is a useful accessory. Its function is to hold sheets or books of music in a position to allow them to be read easily by the musician. It consists of a base upon which the music can stand, a back against which the music can lean, and a mechanism that will hold the back at the proper angle when raised and yet permit it to be lowered for storage. Ideally, the angle when raised should be 15 to 20 degrees from an imaginary line perpendicular to the base of the desk.

There are two types of music desks. The most common one is either a solid or an open fretwork back hinged to either the nameboard or the wrest plank; the less common one is based upon the pantograph. The latter consists of a series of pivoting slats that fold down into a very compact form when not in use. Regardless of the type selected, the music desk usually is constructed from the same hardwood used for the harpsichord case. The hinges and desk support can be standard piano hardware modified where necessary to fit the smaller harpsichord music desk.

Some harpsichord-makers combine the music desk with a base that covers the nut and tuning pins and, in addition, serves as the jack rail. This system, illustrated in Figure 35, offers the advantages of simple construction and easy access for tuning and adjustment; it also keeps dust out of the harpsichord mechanism.

The Lid. The lid of the harpsichord serves two purposes. First, when closed, the lid prevents dust and dirt from entering the instrument where it could cause damage to the action. Second, when open, the lid acts as a reflector, directing the sound from the strings outward to the listener rather than upward to the ceiling.

Depending upon the design of the case, there are two different types of lids used on harpsichords. In the first type, for harpsichords with square cheeks (Figure 3), the lid is flat and there is a removable panel covering the opening in front of the keys. This panel is held in place with pegs on the bottom edge and rabbets in the two cheeks. In the second type, for harpsichords with slanted cheeks (Figure 7), there is no removable panel; instead, the forward portion of the lid slopes downward over the keyboard.

This latter harpsichord lid is designed so that it can be opened in three stages (Figures 33, 34, 35). In the first stage, only the keyboard cover is folded back, exposing the keyboard. In the second stage, the keyboard cover and the first panel are folded back, exposing the music desk as well as the keyboard. In the third stage, the second panel with the folded-back keyboard cover and the first panel on top of it is raised and held in position with the lid support. This exposes the strings, the soundboard, the music desk, and the keyboard.

32. Harpsichord Case Closed

33. *Harpsichord Case Partially Open*

34. *Harpsichord Case Partially Open*

35. Harpsichord Case Fully Open

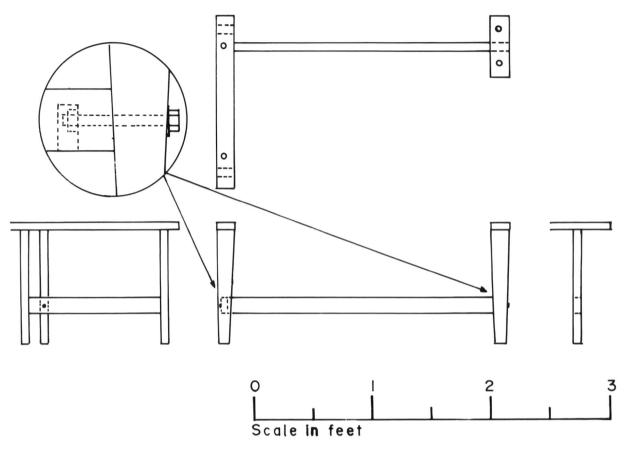

36. *Plan for Trestle Stand*

37. *View of Trestle Stand*

38. View of Contemporary Stand

The Stand. The function of the harpsichord stand is to support the instrument so that the keys are at a convenient playing height. This height has not been standardized and varies from 28 to 30 inches depending upon the designer or the musician for whom the instrument is intended.

There are two different types of stands used. The first is simply three or more legs that are secured with plates to the bottom of the harpsichord case. The second is the trestle (Figures 36 and 37), in which the legs are connected to one another by braces, and the whole assembly is then secured to the bottom of the harpsichord case with bolts. Whichever system is chosen, the primary requirement other than holding the harpsichord at the proper height is that the support be sturdy and wobble free. For this reason the trestle stand is probably superior to independent legs. If, however, portability is a desirable aspect of the design, then separate legs should be considered, for they are easily demounted. As with the other accessories, the wood used for the stand is the same as that used for the harpsichord case.

The harpsichord stand shown in Figure 38 was designed to impart a contemporary appearance to the instrument. The stand is constructed so that it can be removed from the harpsichord, disassembled, and stored flat to facilitate transporting the instrument from one location to another.

PART II.

The Design of the Harpsichord

There are no secrets to the design of the harpsichord. All of its parts and pieces function according to the laws of physics. The keys are simple levers. The jacks, whose plectra displace the strings by brute force, are merely extensions of the key levers. The strings, on displacement, vibrate in the same way as all plucked strings. The soundboard and sound box, functioning as a resonator, respond to the vibrations of the strings, reinforcing them so that they may be heard. However, saying that there are no secrets to the design of the harpsichord is not the same as saying all harpsichords are alike. Harpsichords differ from one another in the same ways and for the same reasons that automobiles differ from one another or houses differ from one another. That is, the designs of harpsichords vary, and the quality of construction of harpsichords varies. The good harpsichord starts with a good design, uses appropriate materials, and is well constructed. The poor harpsichord may lack one or all of these characteristics.

A good harpsichord is remarkable, because the strings, jacks, keys, and sound box all work in harmony with one another. The strings should sound crisp, clear, and of equal volume across the entire range of the instrument. The jacks should pluck precisely and cleanly, return promptly, and dampen effectively. The keys should work effortlessly and noiselessly. The sound box should reinforce the most desirable frequencies and filter out the rest. In addition, the good harpsichord should be handsome to look at and a pleasure to play. Finally, it should be an instrument on which the appropriate music will sound the way it was intended to sound and never as if the music would sound better if played on a different instrument. Good harpsichords do not just happen. They are designed and built to be good.

In designing a harpsichord, several general objectives must be kept in mind. These are:

1. The range and disposition of the harpsichord should be capable of encompassing the major portion of the music written for the instrument.
2. The acoustical design of the harpsichord should produce the desired sound quality or characteristics as well as the necessary volume for its intended purposes.
3. The visual design of the harpsichord should be compatible with the designer's personal sense of aesthetics.
4. The physical design of the instrument should facilitate the playing of the harpsichord and, additionally, should be within the capabilities of the instrument-maker.

Decisions made about how each of these objectives should be achieved will be reflected in the acoustical and visual structure of the instrument. These decisions also will result in specifications for the harpsichord that define such characteristics as the compass, scale, and size of the instrument. From the specifications, the plans for the instrument can be drawn.

In the sections that follow, such specifications for a harpsichord will be developed. A summary of these specifications is presented here for convenience.

Compass: five octaves, FF to f^3
Registration: two eight-foot plus a harp stop
Octave span: 6 1/4 inches
String scale: c^2 = 12 inches
String gauge: c^2 = .011 inches (#2) steel wire
Number of manuals: one
Overall length: approximately 84 inches

Drawing the String Plan

The design of the harpsichord begins with the drawing of the string plan. The string plan is a drawing that shows the length of each string to be used in the instrument. It also shows the point where the jacks are to pluck the strings as well as the placement of the strings in relation to one another.

TABLE 5							
THEORETICAL STRING LENGTHS*							
Note	String Length	Note	String Length	Note	String Length	Note	String Length
f^3	4.872	$c^{\#2}$	11.381	$a^\#$	25.214	G	55.865
e^3	5.137	c^2	12.000	a	26.587	$F^\#$	58.904
$d^{\#3}$	5.416	b^1	12.653	$g^\#$	28.036	F	62.164
d^3	5.711	$a^{\#1}$	13.341	g	29.558	E	65.549
$c^{\#3}$	6.022	a^1	14.067	$f^\#$	31.166	$D^\#$	69.114
c^3	6.349	$g^{\#1}$	14.834	f	32.891	D	72.570
b^2	6.695	g^1	15.639	e	34.682	$C^\#$	76.836
$a^{\#2}$	7.059	$f^{\#1}$	16.490	$d^\#$	36.568	C	81.015
a^2	7.443	f^1	17.403	d	38.397	BB	85.422
$g^{\#2}$	7.848	e^1	18.350	$c^\#$	40.654	$AA^\#$	90.066
g^2	8.275	$d^{\#1}$	19.348	c	42.865	AA	94.971
$f^{\#2}$	8.725	d^1	20.316	B	45.197	$GG^\#$	100.147
f^2	9.208	$c^{\#1}$	21.510	$A^\#$	47.654	GG	105.585
e^2	9.709	c^1	22.680	A	50.249	$FF^\#$	111.329
$d^{\#2}$	10.237	b	23.914	$G^\#$	52.988	FF	117.490
d^2	10.794						

* c^2 = 12 inches, octave multiplier 1.89, semitone multiplier 1.0544.

The process of drawing the string plan begins with developing the table of theoretical lengths for each string in the harpsichord. For this it will be necessary to know the range of the instrument, the string scale, and the multipliers that will be used. For reasons *discussed earlier* (See Part I, The Compass of the Harpsichord), a range of FF to f^3 and a string scale of c^2 = 12 inches would be desirable. Further, by using the octave multiplier 1.89 (semitone multiplier 1.0544) instead of doubling the string length for each octave, it will be found that, in addition to a uniform progression of wire-size changes (one gauge per octave), there will be fewer strings

in the bass section that need to be foreshortened. Using this information, the string lengths given in Table 5 can be developed.

If, for example, the overall length of the instrument is to be approximately 84 inches, the next step would be to determine how much of this 84 inches would be consumed by such things as the keys, lock board, nameboard, tuning pins, case, etc., and what remains to be used for the strings. This information is needed to draw the string plan.

Experience has shown that 1/2-inch plywood is an appropriate material from which to build the case of a single manual harpsichord. Consequently, this dimension will be used whenever dealing with a component of the case. Also, since there will be two eight-foot choirs of strings, two rows of tuning pins will be needed. Depending on the height of the nut, the minimum amount of space needed for the tuning pins will vary from 2 1/2 to 3 inches. The latter dimension will be used, since it results in a less acute string angle between the nut and the tuning pin. This will make the tuning of the instrument easier and will lead to fewer broken strings. Thus, from the keyboard end of the case to the nut, the following space requirements must be provided (refer to Figure 2 for the location of each part):

Thickness of lock board	1/2 inch
Distance between lock board and key slip	1 inch
Clearance between key slip and key	1/8 inch
Length of front of key	5 inches
Clearance between key and nameboard	1/8 inch
Thickness of nameboard	1/2 inch
Space between nameboard and nut	3 inches
Total	10 1/4 inches

At the tail of the harpsichord it will be necessary to allow about 4 inches of space between the bridge and the sides of the case and

1/2 inch for the thickness of the case, for a total of 4 1/2 inches. However, because the tail makes an acute angle with the spine, about 2 1/4 inches should be added to accommodate the extra length created by this angle. These figures give:

Lock board to nut	10 1/4 inches
Bridge to tail	4 1/2 inches
Extra for tail angle	2 1/4 inches
Total	17 inches

Since the overall length of the instrument is to be approximately 84 inches, by subtracting 17 inches from this figure it will be found that the length of the longest string (FF) should be 67 inches. Having found the length of the longest string and taking the length of the shortest string from Table 5—that is, f^3 = 4.872—the plucking points can be established and, hence, the position of the nut on the wrest plank as well as the width of the wrest plank.

As explained earlier, it is virtually impossible to pluck the strings of the harpsichord in the bass and treble sections at the ideal distance of one-seventh of their length. One-tenth in the bass and one-half in the treble are the more usual plucking distances. For the instrument being designed, this would make the plucking point for FF at 6.7 inches from the nut and the plucking point of f^3 at 2.43 inches from the nut. These two dimensions can be rounded off to 6 3/4 and 2 7/16 inches respectively.

With these figures it now is possible to lay out the string plan. For this the following items are required:

> Drawing pencil and eraser
> Carpenter's square
> Three-foot rule graduated in six-teenths of an inch
> Six-foot straightedge
> Drawing paper 40″ × 90″
> String-spacing gauge

The string-spacing gauge must be made. This will require a rectangular piece of cardboard about 3 inches wide by 8 1/4 inches long. Measure in 1 inch from the end of a long side and make a mark *A* with a pencil. Measure over from this mark exactly 6 1/4 in-

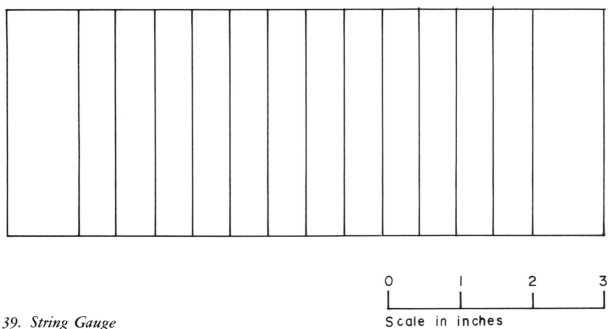

39. *String Gauge*

0   1   2   3

Scale in inches

ches and make a second mark *B*. Divide the space between *A* and *B* into twelve equal spaces. The easiest way to do this is to lay the piece of cardboard at an angle on a ruled sheet of tablet paper and adjust the angle until there are exactly twelve spaces between the two marks on the cardboard as shown in Figure 39. Mark the edge of the cardboard at the intersection of it and the lines on the paper, and draw lines perpendicular to the long side across the width of the cardboard.

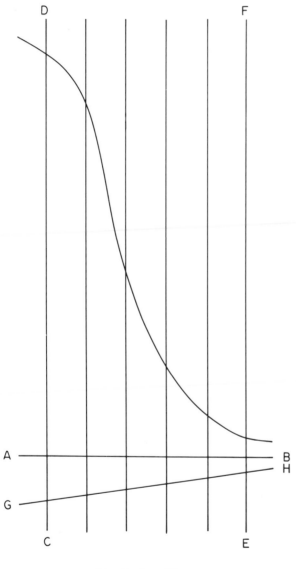

40. String Plan

Begin laying out the string plan by drawing line *AB* across the drawing paper 18 inches in from the bottom edge and exactly perpendicular to the long side. (Refer to Figure 40 as these and subsequent instructions are followed.) Line *AB* represents the plucking point of the strings. Draw a second line *CD* the length of, parallel to, and 4 inches in from the left-hand side. Make sure that this line is precisely perpendicular to line *AB*. Use a square to ascertain this. Line *CD* represents the position of the lowest bass string (FF). Draw a third line *EF* parallel to and 31 1/4 inches from line *CD*. Line *EF* represents the position of the highest treble string (f³).

Measure down 6 3/4 inches from line *AB* along line *CD* and make a mark *G*. Measure down 2 7/16 inches along line *EF* and make a mark *H*. Connect mark *G* to mark *H* with a straight line. Line *GH* represents the position of the nut on the wrest plank in relation to the plucking points.

Measure 67 inches up from mark *G* along line *CD* and make a mark *I*. The distance between *G* and *I* represents the length of the longest bass string. Draw a line perpendicular to line *CD* through point *I* until it intersects line *EF*. Make a mark *J*. Line *IJ* should be exactly 31 1/4 inches long if the measurements are accurate.

Using the string-spacing gauge, mark 60 spaces across line *IJ*. Repeat the process, marking out 60 spaces across line *AB*. In both cases there should be no discrepancies between the length of the lines and their division into 60 spaces. With a straightedge, connect the marks on line *IJ* with those on line *AB*, extending the lines so that they intersect the nut *GH*.

Number the lines from left to right, beginning with *CD* as number 1 and EF as number 61. Using the Table of Theoretical String Lengths (Table 5), lay out the length of each string, measuring upward from the nut *GH*. Be sure to measure from the nut rather than the plucking points. Thus, measure 4

7/8 inches from *GH* along line number 61 (*CD*) and make a mark; measure 5 1/8 inches from *GH* along line number 60 and make a second mark. Continue in this fashion until the theoretical length exceeds the distance between line *GH* and line *IJ*.

Connect the mark on line number 61 to the mark on line number 60. Connect the mark on line number 59 to the mark on line number 58. Continue in this manner until line *IJ* is reached. These connected lines represent the centerline of the bridge on the soundboard. The remaining strings in the bass section as well as some of those already drawn must be foreshortened.

The amount of foreshortening will depend upon the final desired shape of the tail of the harpsichord. The tail could be at a right angle to the spine of the harpsichord, in which case the bridge line would resemble that on the right in Figure 41; the tail could make an acute angle with the spine, in which case the bridge line would resemble that on the left in Figure 41. This latter form is more elegant and will be used in completing the layout of the string plan.

To lay out the bridge line to accommodate a tail that makes an acute angle, begin by drawing a line through mark *I* at an angle of 60 degrees (although other angles would be equally appropriate). Extend the line until it intersects the bridge line. Join the two lines with a smooth, flowing, curved line. The best way to make this line is to use a thin, flexible strip of wood or metal, bending it to the desired curvature and drawing along its edge. (The help of a second person will make this step easier.) All of the strings falling between this curve and the last bass string are shorter than their theoretical length. As a consequence, these strings must be foreshortened and formed from a heavier gauge wire than otherwise would have been the case. The process of foreshortening already has been discussed. What follows is the application of this process to the development of the actual

41. Square-tailed and Slant-tailed Harpsichords

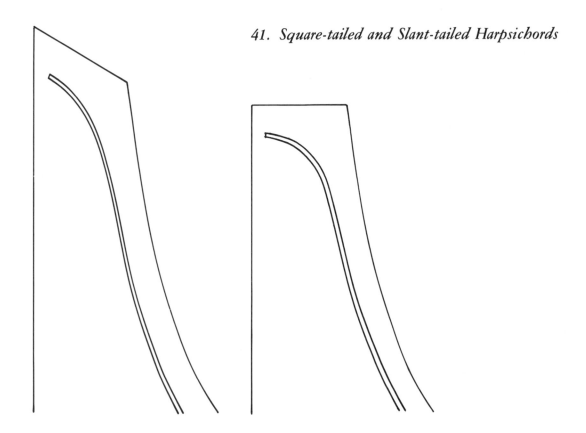

string list that will be used in stringing the harpsichord.

The theoretical string list was based on the decision to change the size of the strings of the instrument one gauge for each octave. Therefore, if c^2 is to be formed from .011-inch or 2-gauge music wire, then the string list without foreshortening would be as follows:

$$f^3 \text{ to } c^3 = 1 \text{ ga.}$$
$$b^2 \text{ to } c^2 = 2 \text{ ga.}$$
$$b^1 \text{ to } c^1 = 3 \text{ ga.}$$
$$b \text{ to } c = 4 \text{ ga.}$$
$$B \text{ to } C = 5 \text{ ga.}$$
$$BB \text{ to } FF = 6 \text{ ga.}$$

However, from G downward the strings must be foreshortened. This requires recalculating the size of wire to be used for each string according to the amount of foreshortening involved. Begin by making a list of the strings to be foreshortened. In the first column of this list indicate the string's theoretical length. In the second column indicate the string's theoretical wire size. In the third column indicate the string's actual length, and in the fourth and final column indicate the actual size of wire to be used in stringing the instrument. As noted earlier, the calculation of the actual wire size involves squaring the diameter of the theoretical wire size, multiplying the square by the theoretical string length, dividing this product by the actual string length, and taking the square root of this sum to determine the diameter of the actual wire size. As an example, for FF with a theoretical length of 117.490 inches, a theoretical wire size of .016 inch, and an actual length of 67 inches, square .016, multiply by 117.490, divide by 67, and then take the square root. The result is .0212 inch. However, 8-gauge wire is .020 inch in diameter and 9-gauge wire is .022 inch in diameter. Since .0212 inch is closest to .022 inch, 9-gauge wire should be used. Continuing this process for all of the foreshortened strings will produce the string list given in Table 6.

TABLE 6

STRING LIST

Non-foreshortened Strings:

Note	String Length	Wire Size	Note	String Length	Wire Size	Note	String Length	Wire Size
f^3	4.872	.010	$c^{\#2}$	11.381	.011	$a^\#$	25.214	.013
e^3	5.137	.010	c^2	12.000	.011	a	26.587	.013
$d^{\#3}$	5.416	.010	b^1	12.653	.012	$g^\#$	28.036	.013
d^3	5.711	.010	$a^{\#1}$	13.341	.012	g	29.558	.013
$c^{\#3}$	6.022	.010	a^1	14.067	.012	$f^\#$	31.166	.013
c^3	6.349	.010	$g^{\#1}$	14.834	.012	f	32.891	.013
b^2	6.695	.011	g^1	15.639	.012	e	34.682	.013
$a^{\#2}$	7.059	.011	$f^{\#1}$	16.490	.012	$d^\#$	36.568	.013
a^2	7.443	.011	f^1	17.403	.012	d	38.397	.013
$g^{\#2}$	7.848	.011	e^1	18.350	.012	$c^\#$	40.654	.013
g^2	8.275	.011	$d^{\#1}$	19.348	.012	c	42.865	.013
$f^{\#2}$	8.725	.011	d^1	20.316	.012	B	45.197	.014
f^2	9.208	.011	$c^{\#1}$	21.510	.012	$A^\#$	47.654	.014
e^2	9.709	.011	c^1	22.680	.012	A	50.249	.014
$d^{\#2}$	10.237	.011	b	23.914	.013	$G^\#$	52.988	.014
d^2	10.794	.011						

* c^2 = 12 inches, octave multiplier 1.89, semitone multiplier 1.0544.

Foreshortened Strings:

Note	Theoretical String Length	Theoretical Wire Size	Actual String Length	Actual Wire Size
G	55.865	.014	56.000	.014
F#	58.904	.014	58.125	.014
F	62.164	.014	59.375	.014
E	65.549	.014	60.625	.014
D#	69.114	.014	61.750	.014
D	72.570	.014	62.750	.014
C#	76.836	.014	63.500	.016
C	81.015	.014	64.125	.016
BB	85.422	.016	64.750	.018
AA#	90.066	.016	65.375	.018
AA	94.971	.016	65.875	.020
GG#	100.147	.016	66.250	.020
GG	105.585	.016	66.625	.020
FF#	111.329	.016	66.875	.020
FF	117.490	.016	67.000	.022

Designing the Jacks

After the string plan has been drawn, the jacks and associated parts of the harpsichord's action must be designed. Standard sizes of materials should be incorporated into the design whenever possible, for this will simplify the subsequent fabrication of the parts for the instrument. For example, there is an aluminum channel available at many hardware stores that measures 41/64 inch in width, 1/2 inch in height, and 1/16 inch in wall thickness. It comes in six-foot lengths, which means that one length will make two jack slides. Calculation reveals that the inside width of the channel is 33/64 inch, just right to provide a sliding fit for a jack body 1/2 inch wide. Since aluminum is a relatively easy material for the amateur instrument-maker to work with, the size of available channel can be used to determine the width of the jack body.

The thickness of the jack body can be determined by the available sizes of materials and tools, too, for it must be remembered that slots must be cut across the aluminum jack slides so there will be rectangular openings in the channel to accommodate the jack bodies. If a jack body 3/16 inch thick is used, it will be found that many plastics in sheet form are readily available in this thickness. Additionally, a jack body 3/16 inch thick is less apt to warp or distort.

Two measurements for the jack body now have been determined: it will be 1/2 inch wide and 3/16 inch thick. The length of the jack body is determined by the distance between the top of the key levers and the strings. This distance, in turn, is determined by the depth of the sound box. For a single-manual harpsichord, this depth usually is about 6 inches although, of course, it could be deeper or shallower according to the desires of the designer. In fact, some harpsichord-makers attempt to construct the sound box with dimensions that will cause it to resonate at Middle C and, thus, reinforce the mid-range frequencies more than those at the high and low range of the instrument. It is questionable whether this practice is of any value, since no empirical research has been carried out on the matter. Additionally, most harpsichords will sound good in the middle range regardless of the dimensions of the sound box. It is the bass and treble sections of the harpsichord's compass that are the weakest. However, the quality of sound in these sections is controlled more by the selection of string sizes and plucking points than sound box design.

Using 6 inches as the depth of the sound box, the bottom of the case and the thickness of the key levers, key frame, and balance rail will take up about 2 7/8 inches of space, and since the strings will lie 3/4 inch above the top of the soundboard, a distance of 3 7/8 inches is left between the top of the key lever and the strings. About 1/4 inch of this distance will be taken up by the end-pin screw in the jack, leaving 3 5/8 inches. To this distance another 3/4 inch must be added for the jack to extend above the strings to accommodate the damper and tongue-adjusting screw. This gives a jack body that totals 4 3/8 inches in length.

Next, the guiding system for the lower end of the jack must be determined. A second slotted aluminum channel identical to the jack slide could be used. This would result in a jack with a simple, rectangular body. However, such a jack would be heavier than is necessary. A simpler jack guide to construct (Figure 12), and one that would reduce the jack weight and friction to a minimum, can be achieved by reducing the width of the jack in its lower portion until it approximates a square in cross section, and then, by making the jack guide by drilling holes, the diameter of which is equal to the diagonal measurement of this narrowed portion of the jack. A piece of 1/4-inch-thick plastic will serve well for the jack guide, and, if the holes drilled to fit the jack body are countersunk from both sides, a minimum of friction will be encountered.

The next step is to locate the slot in the jack body where the tongue of the jack is to be fitted. The dimensions and location of this slot are determined by the dimensions and shape of the tongue used. Harpsichord

tongues are available commercially, complete with an integral spring. Since the cutting of the slots for the plectra is a difficult and tedious task, the amateur instrument-maker may want to purchase the tongues already made. If this is the case, the size and location of the slot in the jack body that will receive the tongue will be determined by the size and shape of the tongue purchased. Assuming, however, that the harpsichord-maker wants to construct the tongues rather than purchase them, the following instructions will be appropriate:

The tongue (Figure 42) is 7/8 inch long, 3/16 inch wide, and 1/8 inch thick. Its upper end is beveled at 45 degrees to bear against the tongue-adjusting screw. Just below this bevel, a hole 3/32 inch square is cut through the tongue to hold the leather plectrum. At the bottom end of the tongue, a transverse hole is drilled to receive the axle pin. On the back of the tongue (the side opposite the bevel), a shallow groove is cut to guide the spring that presses the tongue against the tongue-adjusting screw.

Two slots must be located on the jack body. One slot is for the tongue and the second slot holds the damper felt. Because of the slot for the damper, it is necessary to place the slot for the tongue off-center. This slot must be 1/4 inch wide and 1 1/8 inches long to provide sufficient clearance for the tongue. It is located so that the plectrum lies just below the string. The hole for the axle pin also must be located on the drawing of the tongue and the jack body 1/8 inch above the lower end of the tongue.

The slot for the damper should be 1/16 inch wide and long enough so that a piece of damper felt fitted in the slot will just touch the string.

There should be about 1/4 inch of the jack body between the top of the jack and the tongue slot to provide sufficient material for tapping threads to receive the tongue-adjusting screw.

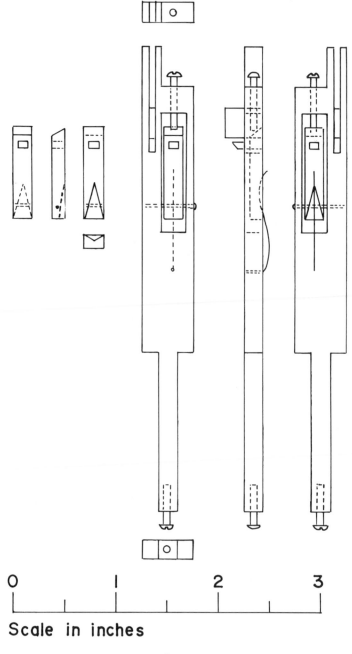

0   1   2   3

Scale in inches

42. *Plan for Jacks*

60

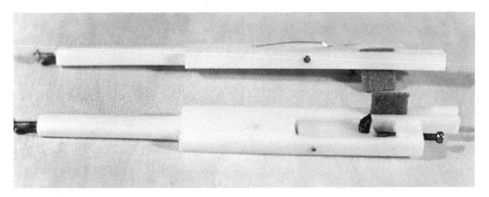

43. *View of Jacks*

44. *Interior View of Wrest Plank Gap*

In addition to the holes for the axle pin and tongue-adjusting screw, holes also must be located for the end screw and the jack spring. The location of these holes is clearly shown in the drawing of the completed jack, Figure 42.

Drawing the Keyboard

After the design of the jack has been decided on, the jack's dimensions can be used to lay out the keyboard. Begin the drawing of the keyboard by determining the length of the key lever. This measurement is obtained by adding up the spaces occupied by the jacks, wrest plank, and nameboard, as well as the clearances that must be provided between the various moving parts. As noted earlier, the playing surface of a harpsichord key (the combined length of the head and tail) is 5 inches. To this measurement, 1/8 inch should be added to allow for clearance between the end of the accidental combs and the nameboard. The nameboard itself should be the same thickness as the sides of the harpsichord case. In this instance the thickness would be 1/2 inch. A space of 3 inches should be left between the nameboard and the nut on the wrest plank to accommodate the tuning pins in the bass section. In the bass section, the distance between the nut and the plucking point along the last string FF is 6 3/4 inches. Since one rank of jacks will be forward of the plucking point and the other rank of jacks back of the plucking point, add the space occupied by one of the jack slides. This would be 41/64 inch plus about 7/64 inch for clearance of the slide in the gap, for a total of 3/4 inch. The overall length of the key lever, then, is 16 1/8 inches, the total of these measurements.

The height of the key lever above the bottom of the harpsichord case is determined in a similar manner by adding the space required for the various parts of the key frame. The bottom of the harpsichord case will be constructed from 1/2-inch plywood. To this measurement 1/4 inch must be added for the key-frame runners. The base of the key frame also will be constructed from 1/2-inch plywood. The balance rail is a piece of 2 1/2 inch × 3/4 inch stock. A clearance of 1/16 inch for the balance-rail pin punchings will be necessary. The key lever itself will be constructed from 3/4-inch stock. When these measurements are added, it will be found that the top of the key lever will be 2 5/16 inches above the inner side of the case bottom.

With this information, a cross-sectional drawing can be made of the keyboard and associated jack action. It is customary to make this drawing coincide with the highest treble string, in this case, f^3. For the drawing, a piece of drawing paper about 12 inches x 22 inches will be needed.

Begin the layout of the keyboard by drawing a horizontal line parallel to and 1 inch above a long edge of the paper (this cross-sectional drawing is shown in Figure 7) to represent the bottom edge of the harpsichord case. All other horizontal lines will be drawn in relationship to this line. Draw a second line 1/2 inch above and parallel to the first line to represent the thickness of the bottom of the harpsichord case. Draw a third line 3/4 inch above and parallel to the first to represent the runners for the key frame. Draw a fourth line 1 1/4 inches above and parallel to the first to represent the base of the key frame. Draw a fifth line 2 1/16 inches above and parallel to the first to represent the bottom edge of the key lever. Draw a sixth line 2 13/16 inches above and parallel to the first to represent the top of the key lever. Draw a seventh line 4 1/2 inches above and parallel to the first to represent the bottom of the wrest plank. Finally, draw an eighth line 6 inches above and parallel to the first to represent the top of the wrest plank, jack slides, and soundboard.

About 3 inches in from the right-hand side of the paper, draw a vertical line between the inside edge of the case bottom and the line representing the top of the soundboard. This line represents the backside of the belly rail. All vertical lines will be drawn in relation to it. Draw a second line 3/4 inch to the left and parallel to this first line to represent the front side of the belly rail. Draw a third line 1 1/4 inches to the left and parallel to the first line between the soundboard line and the line representing the bottom edge of the wrest plank. This line represents the front edge of the belly-rail projection. A fourth line 2 3/4 inches to the left, parallel to the first, and running between the soundboard line and the bottom of the wrest-plank line defines the gap and also the back edge of the wrest plank. A fifth line 11 3/4 inches to the left and parallel to the first between the top edge of the soundboard line and the bottom of the wrest-plank line represents the front edge of the wrest plank. A sixth line 17 3/8 inches to the left and parallel to the first between the top of the key-lever line and the bottom of the key-lever line represents the front edge of the key lever. The tail of the key lever can be marked off 16 1/8 inches to the right of the key front.

An examination of any harpsichord or piano keyboard will reveal that the accidental keys are substantially shorter than the natural keys because, were the accidental keys to pivot at the same point on the balance rail as the natural keys when depressed, they would present a steeper angle to the player. This would cause the tails of the accidental keys to rise higher than the naturals, resulting in greater jack travel. Because of these reasons, the balance point of the accidental keys should be located farther to the rear than those for the naturals. The actual amount of difference between the location of the two rows of balance-rail pins is one-half the difference in length between the two different keys. In the present design, the key head is 2 inches long. Thus, the natural keys are 2 inches longer than the accidental keys, and the balance-rail pins for the accidentals are located 1 inch behind the balance-rail pins for the naturals.

In a harpsichord, the balance-rail pins usually are located at the midpoint of each key lever, although they could be placed somewhat to the front or to the rear of this point were a different amount of jack travel desired. In this design the natural key lever is 16 1/8 inches long. Therefore, the balance point of the natural keys is 8 1/16 inches from the rear edge of the keys. The accidental key lever is 14 1/8 inches long, and its balance point is 7 1/16 inches from the rear edge of the keys. Mark these positions on the drawing of the key lever with two vertical lines that extend about 1/4 inch above the top edge of the key lever and about 3/4 inch below the bottom edge of the key lever. The balance rail itself is 2 1/2 inches wide and 3/4 inch thick, located 1/16 inch below the bottom of the key lever. Both edges are chamfered at an angle of about 15 degrees as shown in Figure 2.

The guide pins should be located 2 inches in front of the tail end of the keys to provide adequate clearance for the jacks. They are not staggered, as are the balance-rail pins, but placed in a straight line. The guide pins are drawn in the same fashion as the balance-rail pins but extend 1/2 inch above the top of the key lever. The back rail is 3 inches wide and 9/16 inch thick, located so that its back edge is directly in line with the belly rail and 1/4 inch below the bottom edge of the key lever. A piece of 1 1/2 " × 1/4 " felt lies between the top of the back rail and the bottom of the key lever to silence and soften the descent of the keys.

The key slip is a molding designed to hide the open space between the bottom of the keys and the key frame. It is 1 1/2 inches high, 1/4 inch wide at the top, and 1/2 inch wide at the bottom. A clearance of 1/8 inch should be provided between the front of the key and the back of the key slip. The key slip is fastened to the front edge of the key-frame base.

The front rail is 3 1/4 inches wide and 1/4 inch thick. It is located at the front of the key frame base directly behind the key slip. A 3/16 inch thick strip of felt is glued to it to serve to control the amount of key dip, in this case 3/8 inch. This completes the cross-sectional drawing of the keyboard.

With the information obtained from this drawing and from the string plan, the plan view of the keyboard can be drawn. For this a sheet of drawing paper at least 18″ × 36″ will be needed and, in addition to the regular drawing tools and the string-spacing gauge used in laying out the string plan, a key gauge will be needed. The key gauge must be specially made.

The key gauge (Figure 45) is laid out on a piece of cardboard cut exactly 5 inches wide and 6 1/4 inches long. On this piece of cardboard, one octave of the keyboard will be drawn full size. Begin the drawing by laying out line *AB* lengthwise 2 inches up from the bottom edge of the cardboard. Line *AB* represents the forward edge of the accidental keys. Mark the front edge off into seven equal divisions. Draw perpendicular lines from each mark upward until they intersect line *AB*. Starting at the left, identify each rectangular area for the key it will represent starting with C: C, D, E, F, G, A, B.

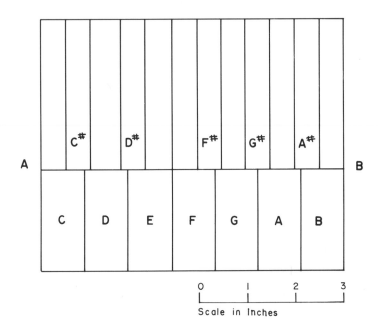

45. *Key Gauge*

Along the centerline *AB* make a mark 3/8 inch to the left and a second mark 1/8 inch to the right of the line between C and D. Connect these two marks with perpendicular lines running to the top edge of the cardboard. The space between the two lines represents the accidental key C#.

Along the centerline AB make a mark 1/8 inch to the left and a second mark 3/8 inch to the right of the line between D and E. Connect these two marks with the upper edge with perpendicular lines. The space between these two lines represents D#.

Extend the line between E and F the full width of the cardboard.

Along the centerline *AB* make marks 3/8 inch to the left and 1/8 inch to the right of the line between F and G. Connect these two marks with perpendicular lines running to the upper edge. The space between these two lines represents F#.

Along the centerline *AB* make marks 1/4 inch to the left and 1/4 inch to the right of the line between G and A. Connect to the upper edge as before. The space between these two lines represents G#.

Along the centerline AB make marks 1/8 inch to the left and 3/8 inch to the right of the line between A and B. Connect to the upper edge as before. The space between these two lines represents A#. This completes the drawing of the key gauge.

For the following instructions for drawing the plan for the keyboard refer to Figure 46. A piece of drawing paper 18″ × 36″ will be needed. Begin by drawing line *AB* 1 inch above and parallel to one of the 36-inch edges of the drawing paper. Line *AB* represents the front edge of the keyboard. Draw a second line *CD* 16 1/8 inches above and parallel to line *AB*. Line *CD* represents the rear edge of the keyboard. Draw line *EF* 2 inches above and parallel to line *AB*. Line *EF* represents the end of the head of the keys. Draw line *GH* 5 inches above and parallel to line *AB*. Line *GH* represents the end of the accidental combs.

Draw a line *IJ* perpendicular to line *AB* connecting with line *CD* 18 inches in from the left hand side of the paper. Line *IJ* represents the division between Middle C and b. Draw line *KL* 6 1/4 inches to the left and parallel to line *IJ*. Draw line *MN* 12 1/2 inches to the left and parallel to line *IJ*. Draw line *OP* 6 1/4 inches to the right and parallel to line *IJ*. Draw line *QR* 12 1/2 inches to the right and parallel to *IJ*. Lines *IJ*, *KL*, *MN*, *OP*, and *QR* divide the keyboard into four octaves.

Using the lines representing the divisions between the natural keys on the key gauge, mark out 4 spaces to the left of *M* on line *AB* and four spaces to the right of *Q* on line *AB*. Divide the space between *M* and *K* on line *AB* into 7 spaces using the key gauge. Repeat for the spaces between *K* and *I*, *I* and

O, *O* and *Q*. Repeat the same marks on line *EF*. Connect the marks on line *AB* to the marks on line *EF* with vertical lines. There should be 37 spaces representing the natural key heads from FF to f³.

Using the key gauge, divide the space between line *MN* and line *KL* along line *GH* into spaces representing the tails of the naturals and the tails of the accidental keys. There should be 12 such spaces. Repeat along line *GH* for the spaces between lines *KL* and *IJ*, *IJ* and *OP*, *OP* and *QR*. To the left of line *MN* along line *GH*, mark out 7 spaces representing FF, FF#, GG, GG#, AA, AA#, and BB. Use the right-hand end of the key gauge for this purpose. To the right of line *QR* along line *GH* mark out 6 spaces representing c³, c#³, d³, d#³, e³, and f³. Use the left-hand end of the key gauge for this purpose.

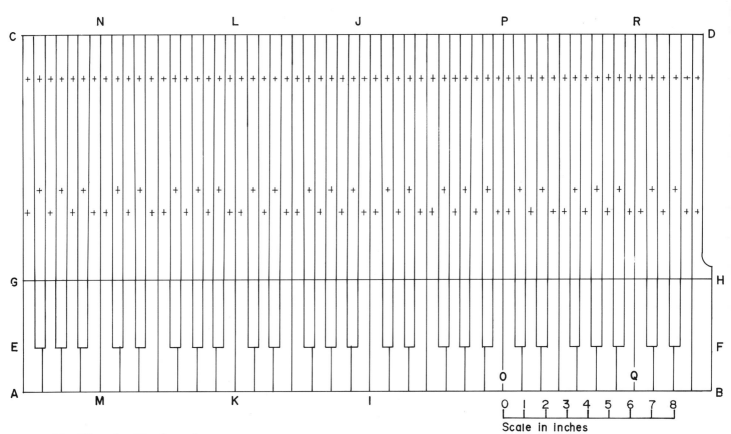

46. *Plan for Keyboard*

Repeat these same procedures along line *EF.* Connect the marks on line *GH* to those on line *EF.*

Using the string-spacing gauge, mark out 7 spaces along line *CD* to the left of mark *N.* Mark out 12 spaces between *N* and *L* along line *CD,* also using the string-spacing gauge. Repeat for the spaces between *L* and *J, J* and *P,* and *P* and *R.* Mark 6 spaces along line *CD* to the right of the mark *R.* These 61 spaces represent the tails of the key levers. Connect the marks on line *GH* to the marks on line *CD.* This outlines the shapes of the 61 key levers. Note that the key levers vary in width back of line *GH.* These variations are necessary due to the irregular spacing of the natural and accidental key combinations.

The final step in drawing the keyboard plan is to locate the position of the balance-rail pins and guide pins. This is easily accomplished from the information taken from the cross-sectional drawing. The only thing to remember in doing this is that the pins should be located in the center of the key levers.

Drawing the Plans for the Case

The jacks, jack slides, and jack guide must be added to the cross-sectional drawing of the keyboard (Figure 7) before the plan for the harpsichord case can be started. The necessary dimensions for these parts were given earlier. After drawing the jacks in place on the keyboard, the jack rail should be drawn in cross-section above the jacks. The bottom edge of the jack rail should be 7/16 inch above the upper ends of the jacks. The felt itself should be 2 inches wide and 1/4 inch thick. The jack rail can be a narrow batten about 3 inches wide and 3/4 inch thick, or it can extend from just in front of the rows of jacks back to the nameboard and become part of the music desk.

Next, the nameboard should be drawn in place. It should be 1/2 inch thick, with its bottom edge parallel to and 1/8 inch above the top of the keys. The back edge of the nameboard should coincide with the front edge of the wrest plank. The nameboard should extend upward so its top edge is 1/2 to 3/4 inch higher than the upper side of the jack rail.

A cross-sectional view of the nut is shown in Figure 16. It should be drawn in the correct position on the wrest plank as measured along string f³ on the string plan. Similarly, a cross-sectional view of the bridge should be drawn in the correct position on the soundboard as measured along string f³ on the string plan. Also, the bottom edge of the soundboard should be drawn in 1/8 inch below its top edge.

The final outline of the front portion of the harpsichord case should be drawn as shown in Figure 7. This will give the harpsichord a sloped front. If a square front is desired, it should be drawn as shown in Figure 3. This completes the cross-sectional drawing of the harpsichord.

Using this drawing as a reference, lay out the position of the belly rail, gap, wrest plank, nameboard, front edge of the keyboard, key slip, and lockboard on the string plan (Figure 40). Extend the lines approximately 3 inches to the left of FF and 3 inches to the right of f³.

The position of the two rows of tuning pins on the wrest plank should be drawn next. This position is found by dividing the wrest plank between the nut and the front edge of the nameboard into three equal spaces. This will result in two lines that run roughly parallel to the nut. The tuning pins for the strings on the treble side of the jacks are located on the line nearest the nut. Those for the strings on the bass side of the jacks are located on the line farthest from the nut.

Locate the position of each tuning pin on its appropriate line by drawing a line at a right angle to the nut from the point where the string intersects the bridge-pin line on the nut to the point where it intersects the line for the tuning pins (Figure 19). Since the nut lies at an angle of about 10 degrees from the perpendicular, this right-angle bend will provide a positive bearing between the string and its bridge pin.

For the soundboard to vibrate freely, there should be three to four inches of soundboard between the bridge and the sides of the harpsichord case, and at least 2 1/2 inches of space between the last string and the sides of the case. Therefore, begin drawing the outline of the harpsichord case by drawing its inner edge. Start by drawing a line parallel to and 2 1/2 inches away from string FF. This line represents the inner edge of the harpsichord spine and should be extended the length of the paper. Draw a second line 3 inches away from and parallel to FF to represent the outside of the spine.

Moving to the far end of the string plan, draw a line parallel to and 4 inches beyond the angled portion of the bridge line to represent the inner edge of the tail. This line should extend from the inside edge of the spine to about 6 inches beyond the curve of the bridge. Draw a second line 1/2 inch away and parallel to the first to represent the outside edge of the tail.

The drawing of the lines to represent the bent side of the harpsichord case will require the use of a long, flexible strip of wood or metal capable of making the necessary curve. The portion of the bent side that joins to the tail of the instrument should be straight, approximately parallel, and no closer than 4 inches to the bridge. As the bent side approaches the sharp curve at the forward end of the soundboard, it too should bend outward and remain approximately parallel and no closer than 4 inches to the bridge. In no case should the bend be too extreme, since this would present problems later when laminating the bent side. Having drawn the line to represent the inner edge, draw a second line 1/2 inch away from the first to represent the outer edge of the bent side.

The short side is drawn in the same way as the spine, allowing 2 1/2 inches between f^3 and the inner edge of the short side. Draw a second line 1/2 inch away from the first to represent the outer edge of the short side.

The liners are drawn next. If preferred, they may be drawn with a dotted line to prevent confusing them with other parts of the harpsichord. The liners are 3/4 inch thick. They extend from the belly rail along the spine to the tail, across the tail to the bent side, down the bent side to the short side and end at the belly rail.

The sound box braces (shown in Figure 28) should be drawn next. Like the liners, they are 3/4 inch thick. Again, dotted lines may be preferred. Begin by bisecting the angle between the spine and the belly rail, so the first brace will run at a 45-degree angle between that corner and the bent side. Next, divide the belly rail into three parts, and draw two more braces at the same angle as the first between the belly rail and the bent side. Finally, divide both the bent side and the spine into three equal parts, and connect the bent side to the spine with braces at each of these divisions.

Three knee braces are needed for the belly rail. These should be equally spaced between the first three braces and at right angles to the belly rail. They should extend about 8 inches into the sound box.

The ribbing of the soundboard (Figure 14) should be drawn next. For this purpose it might be better to use a different color pencil to prevent confusion with the case bracing. The cutoff bar is drawn first. It is 1/2 inch thick and should be placed so that it runs approximately parallel to the straight portion of the bridge, intersecting the belly rail about 15 inches over from the short side. Four braces equally spaced and perpendicular to the spine should be drawn in the triangular area described by the cutoff bar, belly rail, and spine. They are 1/4 inch thick. A sound hole 3 1/2 inches in diameter should be drawn approximately in the center of this triangle but it must not overlap any of the soundboard braces. If desired, the sound hole may be omitted as long as a small opening is made in the bottom of the case to equalize variations in air pressure. This completes the drawing of the sound box portion of the harpsichord.

The position of the keyboard in relation to the sides of the harpsichord is determined next. Place the plan of the keyboard layout over the string plan, and position key FF and key f^3 between the nameboard and the key slip. These keys should be so located that their tails fall directly under the line representing the strings FF and f^3 respectively. Having identified the position of the two end keys, the end blocks may be drawn. They run from the key slip to the nameboard and fill the gap between the sides of the last keys and the harpsichord case. Allow 1/8 inch clearance on the left side of FF and on the right side of f^3.

Complete the drawing of the harpsichord plan by drawing the position of the wrest-plank blocks. These blocks are 1 1/2 inches thick and extend from the back edge of the nameboard to the front edge of the belly rail. Dotted lines can be used to show their position. The drawing of the finished plan should closely resemble the one illustrated in Figure 2. The drawings just completed constitute the working drawings required for the construction of the harpsichord.

PART III.

The Construction of the Harpsichord

Anyone who has ever examined a harpsichord realizes that it is a complex instrument composed of hundreds, even thousands, of separate parts. Because of this complexity, the interested amateur may be deterred from constructing the instrument. It should be kept in mind, though, that these hundreds of parts are, in themselves, relatively simple. For example, the jacks are among the most complex parts of the instrument, but they are simple rectangles of plastic or wood formed by sawing, routing, drilling, and tapping the material into functional devices. What at first may appear to be an overwhelming task can be broken down into a series of simpler tasks, each of which can be mastered by the determined novice.

The builder must understand, however, that the ultimate success of the instrument will depend upon the accuracy with which these many parts are made and fitted together. As an example of this need for accuracy, assume that the strings of a harpsichord being built are evenly spaced at 6 1/4 inches to the octave and that, when cutting the slots in the jack slides, an error of 1/64 inch to the octave developed. This is not a very great error when limited to a single octave, but if the error accumulates for five octaves, it will total 5/64 inch. This amount of discrepancy between the string spacing and the jack spacing will make it difficult to set the jack slides so that the jacks will pluck properly at each end of the scale and still will not touch the strings behind them when moved to the off position. To prevent such errors from developing, special jigs and gauges are used during the construction of the harpsichord. In fact, since the relationship of the jacks to the strings is crucial, the jack slides often are slotted first and then used as a gauge to determine the string spacing on the bridge and nut.

A harpsichord can be built using only hand tools. That is the way most harpsichords were built prior to the twentieth century. The builder today will find that many of the operations involved in the construction of the instrument are accomplished more easily with hand tools than with machine tools. Nevertheless, when multiple holes the same size are to be drilled, when numerous pieces of plastic or wood are to be cut into the same shape, and any time an operation needs to be repeated over and over, machine tools will prove advantageous in terms of speed and accuracy. For this reason, the builder should have access to a table saw, jointer, drill press, and band or jig saw.

The materials used in the construction of the harpsichord should be the best that the builder can afford. This is especially true of the woods used in the soundboard, keyboard, wrest plank, and action. The wood should be well seasoned, straight of grain, and clear of knots or other defects. The wood should be purchased as far in advance of construction as possible and stored in the same room in which the instrument will be built, so it will attain a uniform moisture content.

The hardwood used in the case construction should be selected for grain pattern and color to harmonize with the designer's taste. In this regard, some of the more common hardwoods used in harpsichord construction, ranked according to their relative cost, are as follows:

Rosewood (most expensive)
Walnut
Mahogany
Cherry
Maple
Oak (least expensive)

A good aliphatic-resin wood glue such as Franklin's Titebond or a plastic-resin wood glue such as Weldwood should be used. The aliphatic resin is the easiest of the two to work with and has proven strong and durable in use.

If one can afford it, the hardware used (hinges, bolts, screws, knobs, etc.) should be of solid brass, because of the aesthetic beauty and durability of this metal.

The reader is cautioned to remember that even the best-written book is no substitute for the actual experience of designing and constructing one's own harpsichord. Inevitably, mistakes will be made, but if due care is taken and patience is exercised, the number of mistakes can be minimized and corrected. Perhaps the greatest error that can be made is to defer working out critical problems in the design until after actual construction has begun. At this point, the options are greatly limited by what already has been constructed, whereas, during the design phase any changes needed in the physical structure of the instrument can be accommodated quite easily by simply redrawing the parts affected. In addition, the reader also is cautioned that if there is any question as to whether a specific mechanism, such as the hand stops, will function as planned, it is a good idea to construct a working model of the mechanism and to test it prior to installing it in the harpsichord. Finally, it is worthwhile to recall that some of the early harpsichord-makers purposely omitted one or more of the score marks they were in the habit of scribing across the tops of the natural keys as a reminder that only God is perfect.

Constructing the Case

As mentioned earlier, most modern harpsichord cases are constructed with hardwood plywood. This should be 1/2-inch, five-ply birch of cabinet grade. Two 4′ × 8′ sheets of plywood will be required. The various parts of the instrument should be laid out on these sheets of plywood as shown in Figure 47. In the construction of the case, a 1/4″ × 1/2″ strip of hardwood is glued to the upper edges of the plywood to provide extra durability. All exposed sides of the case, except the bottom, are covered with a hardwood veneer. (Whenever hardwood is specified, it refers to the type of wood selected for the case and stand.)

The bottom edges of the sides of the case are trimmed with a hardwood molding.

Laminating the Bent Side. The bent side, due to its curvature, is the most complex member of the harpsichord case. While it is possible to form the bent side by steaming a solid piece of lumber, a laminated bent side will prove to be much more stable and simpler to make. Because of this, the construction of the case is begun by laminating the bent side.

In the laminating process, thin laminae of wood are glued one to another until a sufficient number have been joined together to provide the desired thickness. Commercial plywood is a good example of the product of this process. To obtain the curvature of the bent side, the laminae are glued together and clamped to a curved mold (Figures 48 and 49) until the glue has set.

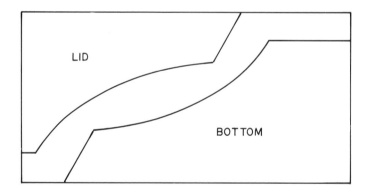

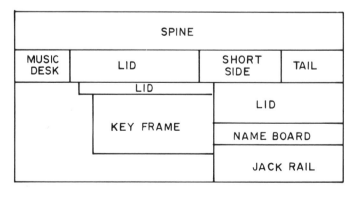

47. *Layout of Plywood*

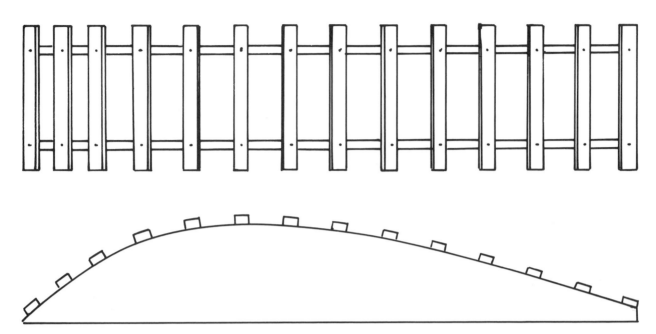

48. *Plan for Bent Side Mold*

When unclamped from the mold, the laminated bent side will retain its curvature; however, there is a tendency for the bent side to spring back slightly upon release from the mold. The amount of springback is difficult to determine since so many variables are present. As a consequence, by beginning the construction of the case with the forming of the bent side, the plans can be modified to accommodate any springback that may occur.

Begin the forming of the bent side by constructing the mold. For this a pattern of the desired curve must be taken from the working drawing. Transfer the curve of the bent side, from the short side to the tail, to a piece of stout cardboard. Draw a second line 3/4 inch shallower than the bent side curve to represent the thickness of the slats that will be attached to the mold sides. Extend this line about 3 inches at both ends to provide extra material in the finished bent side. This will allow for trimming and fitting. Trace the pattern onto a 3/4-inch-thick pine board. (The length and width of this board will be determined by the length and amount of curvature in the bent side.) Cut the board along this curvature with a saber saw, jig saw, or band saw. Using this board as a pattern, cut a second board to the same size and shape.

Lay out along the curvature of each board a series of spaces approximately 5 inches apart. Cut a number of slats of 3/4" × 1 1/2" pine 2 inches longer than the finished width of the bent side. There should be one slat for each space on the mold boards.

Position the slats on the two mold boards so that they overhang the boards by 1 inch on each end. (This overhang will provide places for clamps to be fastened during the lamination process.) Mark and drill each slat to receive #8 × 1 3/4" flathead steel wood screws. Be sure each hole is countersunk to receive the screw. The slats should be trial fitted to the two boards in the previously marked positions. When satisfied with the fit, remove each slat, one at a time, apply glue to the bottom edge of the slat and to the board where the slat is to fit, replace the slat, and tighten the screws. Excess glue should be removed with a damp sponge. This completes the construction of the mold, which may be used as soon as the glue has set.

Measure the length of the bent-side mold along the curve, then cut four pieces of 1/8 inch plywood to this length and to a width 1 inch wider than the desired width of the finished bent side. Trial fit these laminae by clamping all four of them to one end of the mold with C-clamps. If desired, a second slat the same dimensions as the slats used in the mold can be used as a clamping pad. Gently bend the laminae over the mold, clamping with C-clamps and additional slats as you progress.

When satisfied that all four pieces fit correctly and that the clamping arrangement will be adequate, remove the clamps and staple a sheet of wax paper along the length of the mold. This will prevent the laminae from sticking to the mold when they are glued in place. Apply a layer of glue to the upper side of the first and the bottom side of the second piece of plywood. (A small paint roller and paint pan is useful for this process, although a brush can be used instead.) Replace the two pieces of plywood on the mold and proceed to clamp them down in the same way as the trial fit was made. Remove all excess glue with a damp sponge.

After the glue has set, remove the clamps and clamping pads from the mold. Apply a coat of glue to the top piece of plywood on the mold and to the bottom side of the third piece of plywood. Position the parts on the mold, clamp, remove excess glue, and let the glue set. Repeat this procedure for the fourth and final layer of plywood.

It will be noted that as each layer of plywood is added, the amount of springback becomes less and less, so the finished bent side will approximate closely the desired curvature.

50. *Laminating the Bent Side*

When the glue for the fourth lamina has set, the bent side may be removed from the mold to be checked against the drawing. Do not be overly concerned if the curvature varies somewhat from the drawing. This variation is easily adjusted for and will make little difference in the appearance or sound of the finished instrument. Return the glued bent side to the mold, clamping it at both ends so that it can be used as a form for laminating the bent-side linings. Cover one edge of the bent side with a strip of wax paper about 4 inches wide, fastened at both ends with masking tape. Cut six lengths of 1/4″ × 1 1/2″ × 6″ clear pine or spruce. Apply glue to the 1 1/2-inch surface of one of the pieces of wood.

Place a second piece on top of the first and clamp them into position along one edge of the bent side. Use the same clamping procedures as those followed for gluing the bent side. Repeat the procedure for the second lining on the opposite edge of the bent side. Do not forget the wax paper, or the lining may be permanently glued to the bent side before it should be. Repeat the above procedures with the third piece of wood so each lining will be 3/4 inch thick. When the glued linings have set for a sufficient length of time, they and the bent side can be removed from the mold. The mold can be set aside, since it no longer will be needed.

Clean the excess glue from the edges

of the bent side with a scraper. Joint one edge true on the jointer. Measure the finished width of the bent side from the plans, subtract 1/4 inch for the hardwood edging, and cut to width on the table saw. Use a fine-toothed plywood blade, so it will not be necessary to joint this second edge, or, if you do not have such a blade, add 1/16 inch to the sawed width of the bent side and remove this excess material on the jointer.

Scrape the excess glue from the edges of the bent-side linings and joint and saw them to a finished width of 1 1/4 inches.

Fitting and Joining the Case Sides.

From the drawings, measure the lengths and widths of the spine, tail, and short side. Subtract 1/4 inch from the width to allow for the hardwood edging and add 2 inches to each length to allow for fitting the joint. Cut boards from 1/2-inch plywood to these measurements.

The joint that will be used to join the sides of the case to one another is the finger lap joint (Figure 51). It is a very strong joint and will not open up or pull apart under the stress applied to the harpsichord frame. It also is a fairly simple joint to construct.

Starting with the board for the spine, draw a line across the outside of the board at right angles to the side and 1 inch in from the end. With an adjustable bevel, transfer from the plans the angle of the spine to the tail to both edges of the spine board. Connect these two lines with a third line across the inside of the board. There should be a continuous line

completely around the board, with the line on the inner side farther from the end than the line on the outer side.

Lay out an odd number of equal spaces across the line on the inner side. The spaces should be at least 1/2 inch wide but no greater than 1 inch. Connect these spaces to the end of the board using a try square. Continue the lines across the end of the board and down the outer side to connect with the line drawn there. Darken, or X out every other space to represent the material that is to be removed from between the fingers.

With a dovetail saw, cut along each finger, sawing so that the kerf removes material from the waste portion rather than from the finger itself. Do the sawing from the inner side of the board holding the saw at approximately the angle of the tail, so when each cut is finished the kerf touches both the line on the inner and the line on the outer sides of the board. Remove the waste material from between each finger with a wood chisel. Use care in chiseling so each notch is cut square and to the same depth.

Lay the spine board on top and parallel to the tail board, so both outer sides face one another. Mark around the notches very accurately. Lay out the fingers on the tail board in the same manner as for the spine, only in this instance there will be fingers on the tail board where there were notches on the spine. Check the layout very carefully to be certain that they are drawn this way. Saw and chisel out the notches for the fingers on the tail board in the same way as was done on the spine. Be sure all saw cuts are made in the waste material and outside the pencil lines. Again, cut the bottoms of each notch as accurately and as squarely as possible.

Once the fingers of the joint have been formed on both the spine and the tail board, they can be tried for accuracy of fit. The two parts should slide together with firm pressure. Do not use too much force or one of the fingers may break off. If the two parts do not

51. Finger Lap Joint

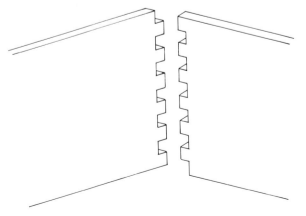

slip together, remove excess wood cautiously where needed. During the trial fits, be sure the two sides stand perpendicular to a level surface. Also, be sure the two sides form the correct angle as shown on the working drawing. Do not trim the ends of the fingers flush until after the sides of the case have been glued together and the bottom of the case is in position.

When satisfied that the joint between the spine and tail has been cut as accurately as possible, move on to the joint between the tail and the bent side. Before marking out this joint, it will be necessary to place the actual bent side in position on top of the plan and mark the curve that it takes in place of the curve originally drawn. After this has been done, proceed to lay out, cut, and fit the tail and bent-side joint in the same manner as the spine and tail joint were made. Again, be sure that all three sides when fitted together stand perpendicular and in the correct relative positions to one another on a level surface. Adjust either joint as necessary to insure a proper fit.

52. Clamping the Finger Lap Joint

Once satisfied with the fitting of the tail and bent-side joint, lay out, cut, and fit the bent side and short side joint. Follow the same procedures that were used for the previous two joints.

Check and recheck the joints by placing the assembled but unglued case sides on top of the plans. Make sure that the spine and the short side lie precisely parallel to one another and the proper distance apart. Also, be sure that when all joints are closed up tightly, the four sides will sit level and square to a flat surface. When satisfied that all of the joints have been fitted correctly, the spine and short side should be cut to their finished length and shape. Remember to subtract 1/4 inch from their length to allow for the edging to be fitted at the keyboard end. Similarly, the angled portion of the spine and short side also should be cut off, again subtracting 1/4 inch for the edgings.

After all of the sides of the case are properly fitted to one another they can be glued together. For these joints an epoxy-resin-type glue should be used because of its strength and because the joint will not need to be clamped as tightly as with other wood glues. Proceed with one joint at a time, beginning with the spine and tail. Simple spring clamps can be used, as shown in Figure 52, to hold the joint together while the epoxy resin sets.

The remaining two joints can be glued and clamped in much the same way. The important thing to remember is to check each clamping setup before gluing to be sure the sides are perpendicular to and level with the work surface and to be certain the clamping procedure will work. Always handle the partially completed case carefully to avoid damaging previously glued joints.

Adding the Belly Rail, Liners, and Bottom.
When the four sides of the case have been glued together, the belly rail can be cut to size and glued in place. The belly rail can be built

up by gluing a length of 1/2″ × 1 1/2″ pine stock to another length of 3/4″ × 8″ pine stock to form the cross section shown on the plan. After the glue has set, the top edge of the belly rail should be jointed and the inner edge beveled as shown in Figure 7. Next the belly rail should be cut to the exact width and length given on the working drawing. Mark the position of the belly rail on the inside of both the spine and the short side. Clamp the belly rail temporarily in position, using small brads driven through the sides of the case and into the ends of the belly rail. Do not drive the brads all the way in or difficulty will be experienced in removing them. Remember to fit the belly rail 1/2 inch above the bottom edges of the sides to allow room for the bottom board to be set in.

Check the fit of the belly rail to be sure that it is at right angles to both the spine and the short side, that it is perpendicular to the work surface, and that it is in the correct position as indicated on the working drawing. When satisfied with the fit, drill pilot holes through the sides of the case and into the ends of the belly rail to receive #6 × 1 1/4″ flathead steel wood screws. (A special countersink-counterbore drill will be found convenient for this and subsequent drilling operations. These are available by screw size at most hardware stores.) There should be three screw holes spaced two inches apart on each side. Put the screws in position and drive them in. Remove the brads from each side. Recheck the fit of the belly rail to be sure that it is in the correct position. When satisfied, remove the screws, apply glue to both ends of the belly rail and to the spine and short side where the belly rail fits. Reposition the belly rail, and drive the screws in tightly. Once again check to be sure everything is square and perpendicular. Remove excess glue. Let the glue set.

The bottom liners should be cut from 3/4″ × 1 1/2″ pine stock. Simple butt joints can be used. Begin with the spine and work around to the short side, fitting, gluing, and clamping the liners in place. The bottom liner should be fitted 1/2 inch above the inside bottom edges of the case to allow space for the bottom board. The liners are fitted only inside the sound box area and not in the area occupied by the keyboard. Short brads can be used to hold the liners in place while the clamps are being applied. Recheck each liner after clamping to be sure it is in the proper position. Remove excess glue.

After the bottom liners have been glued into place, the bottom board can be fitted. The bottom board is cut from a single piece of 1/2-inch plywood. Place the partially completed case on top of the piece of plywood so the inner edge of the spine is parallel to and just over one edge of the plywood. The spine will have to be blocked up with 1/2-inch pieces of scrap to do this. Carefully trace around the outside edge of the case on the remaining three sides and mark the ends of the spine and short side (the inner edge of the case is obscured by the linings). Be sure the case is square with the belly rail before marking. Remove the case from the sheet of plywood.

Redraw the tail, bent side, and short side on the piece of plywood 1/2 inch inside the traced marks so the finished bottom board will fit inside the case. Mark the keyboard end of the piece of plywood 1 1/4 inches shorter than the total length of the case. Cut the bottom board out of the sheet of plywood. A saber saw will be found useful for cutting the curve of the bent side. All other cuts can be made with a hand saw or portable circular saw.

Turn the harpsichord case upside down. Lay the bottom board in position on the bottom liners. Remove any excess wood that may cause binding or distortion. Hold the bottom board temporarily in position with short brads driven through the sides of case into the edges of the bottom board. Do not drive the brads in all of the way. Carefully turn the whole assembly right-side up and check the squareness of the case. Make any adjustments necessary in the bottom board to insure accuracy of fit. When satisfied with the fit of the bottom board, turn the assembly upside down once again. Drill pilot holes for #6 × 1 1/4″ flathead steel wood screws about 6 inches apart through the bottom board into the liners and belly rail. Also drill pilot holes the same size spaced 4 inches apart through the spine and short side into the edges of the bottom board in the area in front of the belly rail. Use care in centering these holes so the screws will not break out of the plywood. Remove the bottom from the sides of the case, and dust out all chips and sawdust from the corners around the liners. Apply a generous coat of glue to the edges of the liners and belly rail and to the forward edges of the spine, short side, and bottom board. Reassemble and drive all of the screws in tightly. A brace with a screwdriver bit will be found convenient for this operation. (Driving the screws about two-thirds of the way in with a hammer will speed up the process and increase the holding power of the screws.) Remove excess glue from both the outside and the inside the case and allow the glue to set.

Mark the position of the soundboard liners on the inside of the case. Cut the liners to fit in the same manner as that used with the bottom liners. Use extra care to insure good joints at each corner so the liners will present a continuous surface for gluing the soundboard. Glue and clamp the liners in place. If the clamps are not deep enough to reach the liners, #6 × 1 1/4″ flathead steel wood screws spaced four to six inches apart may be substituted. Be sure the screw heads are sunk completely below the surface of the plywood sides. Do not remove the screws after the glue has set. They will become a permanent part of the case.

Fitting the Braces. Using information taken from the working drawings, mark out the position of the braces on the inside of the harpsichord case. Each brace should be cut from 3/4″ × 6″ pine stock. Fit the braces to the inside of the case, carefully notching them so they are flush both with the liners and the sides of the case. It is very important that the braces be fitted accurately since they impart much of the strength to the case. Finish the braces to the general shape shown in Figure 30. The upper edges where they meet the belly rail and sides should lie 1/2 inch below the uppermost edge of the liner so they will not interfere with the soundboard. Be sure, also, that the cutaway portion of the braces where the cutoff bar of the soundboard will cross is at least 1/2 inch lower than the height of the cutoff bar.

Glue the bottom braces into position, using screws through the sides, belly rail, and bottom for clamping pressure. Do not remove the screws after the glue has set. They will provide added strength to the joints.

Carefully trim off the excess length of the fingers on the finger joints using a saw, chisel, and wood rasp. Be sure, while doing this, that the corners remain perpendicular to the bottom and flush with the sides. Do not use sandpaper on the joints, because this will round them off.

Installing the Lock Board. The last step in the construction of the harpsichord case prior to veneering it is the installation of the lock board, which is cut from hardwood to the cross section shown in Figure 7. The lock board should fit the entire width of the harpsichord as measured from the outside edge of the spine to the outside edge of the short side. Notches 1/2 inch deep must be cut into the ends of the lock board so it can fit into the case. When cut to size, glue and clamp the lock board to the bottom board of the harpsichord case.

Prepare four strips of 1/4″ × 1 1/2″ pine to fit the bottom of the case between the lock board and the belly rail. These strips will serve to keep the bottom of the keyboard frame level with the top of the lock board. Glue the strips into position so the two outside runners will fall just under the outer edges of the key frame. Space the other two runners equally between the outer two. Small brads can be used to hold the runners down until the glue sets, then countersink the brads and fill the holes with a crack filler such as Durham's Rock Hard Water Putty. Sand off the surplus filler when it is hard.

Veneering the Case. The outer plywood surfaces of the harpsichord case, as well as the two inner cheeks and the area above the soundboard liners are covered with veneer. Fill any depressions or cracks in the harpsichord case with crack filler. Also cover the heads of all the screws with crack filler. When dry, sand the crack filler flush with the surface of the plywood and lightly sand the entire case in preparation for applying the veneer.

Cut 1/4″ × 1/2″ strips of hardwood and fit them to the upper and front edges of the harpsichord case, using mitered joints. If desired, the strips may be cut slightly wider than 1/2 inch and trimmed to fit the sides of the case after they have been glued in place. Glue the strips to the edges, using three-way edging clamps or small brads to hold them until the glue sets. If brads are used, after the glue has set they should be countersunk and the holes filled with a plastic-wood mixture that matches the color of the hardwood being used.

The edging for the top of the bent side must be cut from a wider piece of 1/4-inch hardwood. If necessary, several narrow pieces can be glued to each other at a shallow angle to provide a large enough blank from which to cut the curved strip.

Be certain that the edging strips are flush with both the inner and outer sides of the harpsichord case. If not, trim them to fit with a small plane. Alternatively, a router equipped with a ball-bearing flush-trimming laminate bit can be used. This same router and bit combination can be used to trim the veneer later.

There are three steps involved in veneering the harpsichord case: (1) preparing the veneer, (2) applying the veneer, and (3) trimming the veneer. These same steps also are followed in veneering the lid and other parts of the harpsichord.

The standard thickness of veneer is 1/28 inch. However, some veneers are furnished in 1/20 inch, 1/40 inch, 1/42 inch, and other thicknesses. Veneer ranges in width from a few inches to a foot or more and in length up to eight or more feet. When a quantity of veneer is bought, it usually is matched; that is, each sheet is sold in the same sequence as it was cut from the log. As a result, any two adjoining sheets will have almost identical grain patterns and color. However, there are subtle differences that occur from sheet to sheet as one progresses through a flitch of veneer. For a professional-looking finished product, it is important to keep and use the veneer in the sequence in which it has been sawed. This will, of course, result in some waste, for two full sheets of veneer may be required to cover a surface that would in area require only one-and-one-half sheets. Consequently, it will be prudent to purchase at least thirty percent more veneer than anticipated.

As just suggested, it frequently is necessary to join two or more sheets together to get the necessary width for a particular surface. This is especially true in veneering the lid of the harpsichord. Because veneer is so thin, it is not practical to try to true the edge of a sheet of veneer on the jointer. Instead, another method must be used. One simple method is to use a hardwood plank (birch or hard maple) 3/4″ × 10″ to 12″ × 8′ as a guide. Joint one edge of the plank absolutely straight. Lay the plank on top of the workbench so one long edge overhangs the workbench by about an inch. Lay the sheets of veneer that are to be jointed on top of this plank so their edges overhang the plank by about 1/8 inch or just enough so no uneven portion of the edges will remain when the veneer is cut flush with the edge of the plank. Do not try to joint more than three sheets of veneer at a time. On top of the veneer place a board about 1″ × 4″ × 8′, with its front edge slightly behind the edge of the bottom plank. Clamp the board, veneer, and plank to the top of the workbench, forming a big wooden sandwich. Place the clamps at about 18-inch intervals, using at least three clamps.

Obtain a flush laminate trimming bit with a ball-bearing pilot and secure it in the chuck of a router. Place the router in position on top of the wooden sandwich and adjust it so the ball-bearing pilot will ride against the bottom plank and the cutter against the edge of the veneer. Turn the router on and cut the veneer flush to the plank, except where the router is stopped by the clamps. Remove one clamp at a time and reclamp where the veneer already has been trimmed. Be sure that two clamps always remain in position or the veneer is apt to shift. After reclamping, use the router to cut away the remaining projecting edges of the veneer. Remove the trimmed veneer. If the opposite edges also must be trimmed, turn the stack of veneer around on the plank and joint these edges in the same manner.

After the edges of the veneer are jointed they must be held together with tape while being glued to the harpsichord case. A special gummed veneer tape with a thin paper backing is made for this purpose. Align two of the sheets of veneer on a flat surface, being sure that the grain pattern matches. Using short strips of tape moistened with a wet sponge, join the two sheets together, spacing the tape across the joint at about 12-inch intervals. Next, moisten and apply a single strip of tape over these short pieces of tape along the full length of the joint. Fasten additional sheets to the first two in the same manner un-

til the desired width of veneer is achieved.

When the panels are properly taped together, they can be fitted to the harpsichord case. The inside of the case is veneered first. Begin with the inside curve of the bent side. Cut a piece of veneer to fit the space between the top edge of the bent side and the liner. It should be cut to the exact length and about 1/8 inch wider than the finished width. The veneer can be cut with a sharp knife or with a regular veneer saw. Regardless of the cutting tool used, be sure to use a metal straightedge, such as a carpenter's square, as a guide when making the cut.

The veneer is glued to the plywood case of the harpsichord with contact cement. There are several varieties made especially for veneering purposes. Follow the manufacturer's directions carefully. Apply the necessary coats (usually two) of contact cement to the back of the sheet of veneer and to the inner surface of the bent side. Be careful not to get any of the cement on the liners, since this will interfere with gluing the soundboard in place later. A brush may be used to apply the cement, although a roller similar to those used to apply paint will give a more uniform coating.

The next steps must be followed very carefully because, when the two cemented surfaces come in contact with one another, they must be in the exact position desired as they will bond together instantly. The assistance of a second person is advised.

When the contact cement has completely dried on both surfaces (when the cement is dry a piece of kraft paper should not stick to it), place a piece of kraft paper over the cement-covered bent side. The paper should be slightly larger than the surface it covers. Place the piece of veneer cement-side down on this piece of paper. Position the veneer exactly in respect to the joint at the tail end and to the liner. Slide the piece of paper out from beneath the veneer about 1/4 inch at the tail end. Press the veneer to the case at this point, and it will adhere. (If an error in alignment is made, there is no alternative except to remove the piece of veneer, usually destroying it in the process, clean the remnants of the veneer from the case, and begin again with a new piece of veneer.) Gradually slip the paper from between the surfaces a few inches at a time, pressing the veneer firmly into place. Special rollers are made for this purpose. However, a length of hardwood 3/4″ × 3″ × 10″ with the edges on one end rounded and sanded smooth will be equally useful for applying pressure during the bonding process. Use the piece of wood with a rubbing motion. Work over the veneer several times with the roller or rubber, being careful to work out all air pockets between the veneer and the case.

When the veneer is completely adhered, its upper edge should be trimmed flush with the upper edge of the case. A small plane or a knife with a very sharp blade will work well along the curved surface of the bent side. Finish the trimming with a sanding block, using a fine abrasive paper to remove all traces of cement from the upper edge. Finish veneering the rest of the inside of the harpsichord case in the same way. Do the short side next, followed by the tail section and then the spine. The veneering of the outside of the case should be deferred until after the wrest plank blocks have been glued into place. Then the following sequence of veneering will result in the least visible joints: spine, tail, bent side, and short side.

53. Applying the Veneer

After veneering of the case has been completed, a small molding should be applied around the entire bottom edge of the case. This molding should be made from hardwood similar in cross-section to that shown in Figure 54. When cutting the moldings, make mitered joints at each corner. Glue the moldings to the lower edge of the case, using 3/4-inch brads to hold them in position until the glue has set. Countersink the heads of the brads and fill the nail holes with a matching plastic wood. Rough sand the molding but do not finish sand it or the veneer until after all of the other parts of the harpsichord have been fitted to the case.

54. Cross Section of Molding

55. T Nut Installation

Constructing the Stand

To build the stand, cut the four legs, two lower crosspieces, two upper crosspieces, and the stretcher from hardwood to the dimensions given in Figure 36. The lower crosspieces are attached to the legs with mortise-and-tenon joints. The joined legs then are attached to the upper crosspieces with dowel joints. Use a dowel at least 1 inch in diameter.

A bolt through the lower crosspieces engages a nut inserted into the stretcher through a hole drilled up from the bottom. This technique is illustrated in Figure 36.

The stand is held to the bottom of the harpsichord case with 1/4-inch steel bolts and T nuts. Drill two 1/4-inch holes in the long crosspiece and one 1/4-inch hole in the short crosspiece where shown. Turn the harpsichord case upside down and place the assembled stand on top of the bottom. With the stand in the correct position, mark the location of the three bolt holes. Remove the stand and drill three 3/8-inch holes through the bottom of the case to receive the T nuts. Turn the case right-side up and drive the T nuts in with a hammer. Use two #4 × 1/2″ roundhead steel wood screws driven in at the outer edges of the T nuts to insure the nuts remain in place.

Bolt the harpsichord case to the stand and drill two 1/2-inch-diameter holes through the bottom of the case and 3/4 inch into the long upper crosspiece where shown. Drill two similar holes through the bottom of the case and into the short upper crosspiece. Remove the stand from the harpsichord case and glue 1 1/4-inch lengths of 1/2-inch diameter dowels into the four holes in the crosspieces. Round off the protruding ends of these locating dowels so they will slide easily into the matching holes in the bottom of the case. After the glue has set, the stand should be sanded and all corners rounded slightly in preparation for finishing.

Constructing the Jack Slides and Guide

The jack slides are constructed next, because they will be used as gauges to lay out the position of the bridge pins on the nut and bridge, the tabs on the harp stop, and the guide holes in the jack guide.

The jack slides are made from aluminum channel, which measures 41/64 inch by 1/2 inch with a wall thickness of 1/16 inch. When slotted with a 3/16-inch-thick metal-slotting saw blade, the jack slide will accept jack bodies 3/16 inch thick by 1/2 inch wide.

The slots for the jack slides cannot be cut with an ordinary table saw. Its speed is too great and, usually, its arbor is too small to hold a metal-slotting saw blade. Ideally, the slots should be cut by a milling machine; however, few craftsmen have access to such a piece of equipment. Consequently, the simplest way to accomplish the cutting of the slots is to construct a saw strictly for this purpose. Such a saw can be built easily and inexpensively, using the design given in Appendix 3. The following instructions assume the use of such a saw.

With a hacksaw cut two 36-inch lengths of aluminum channel. Round off any sharp corners and smooth the cut ends with a file. Measure in 2 3/8 inches from one end of one of the lengths and make a line across the top and side of the channel using a scriber and a square.

Clamp the two channels together temporarily (small pieces of double-faced tape will work well) and, using the string spacing gauge, mark out the spacing of the strings on the tops of the two channels, starting with the line previously drawn. Separate the two channels and scribe a line the length of each channel 9/32 inch in from the outside edge.

A 1/4-inch diameter hole is drilled at the intersection of each string line across the channel and the line running the length of the channel. Greater accuracy in the location of these holes can be achieved by drilling a 1/16-inch pilot hole first, followed by the 1/4-inch hole. In drilling the pilot holes, use very light feed pressure when starting the hole, and the drill bit will center itself in the intersection of the two lines scribed on the channel. Once it has centered, normal feed pressure can be used. When all of the 1/4-inch holes have been drilled in both the channels, the holes should be deburred on each side with a countersink. Cut away just enough to chamfer the edges of the holes.

Place the two channels face up on the workbench so the rows of holes are toward the outside of each channel. Slide the channel closest to you 3/16 inch to the right as measured between the centerlines of the holes. Temporarily clamp the two channels in this position and scribe a mark across the face of each channel 1/4 inch in from either end. These marks will serve as alignment guides in the next step.

Unclamp the channels and adhere a length of 1/2-inch-wide double-faced tape to the inner side of one of the channels. Again, place the channels face up on the workbench. Line up the marks at either end and squeeze the sides of the two channels together. Be sure that the two faces are flush with one another. The double-faced tape will hold the two channels in alignment so the slots can be cut in both channels at the same time.

Place a half-inch-square piece of wood about six inches long against the miter gauge on the slotting saw table. Position the joined pair of channels face down and scribed side forward against this piece of wood and align the scribed mark on the forward channel with the saw blade so the saw will cut a slot halfway through the jack clearance holes already drilled in the channels. Check and recheck to be certain that this first slot will be properly cut. Start the saw, drip a little kerosene on the saw blade, and slowly feed the channels past the saw blade.

After the first slot has been cut, remove the wood spacer from in front of the miter gauge and place the slot just cut over the spacing pin. Make a second cut. Repeat this procedure for the remaining slots, being sure to use enough kerosene to prevent the channels from heating up when cutting. After all of the slots have been cut, separate the two channels from one another carefully to avoid bending or distorting them. Deburr the slots with a small file on both the inside and outside edges, being careful not to enlarge the slots in any way. Polish the channels with fine steel wool.

Making the Jack Guide. The jack guide (Figure 12) is cut from a piece of Plexiglas 1/4 inch thick, 2 inches wide, and 34 inches long. Do not remove the protective paper from the plastic, since the layout will be made on this paper. Block the piece of Plexiglas up on a 1/4-inch-thick piece of wood and clamp it and one of the jack slides together. With a square held flush against the side of the jack slide and the blade of the square even with the side of the first slot in the jack slide, draw a line across the Plexiglas with a sharp, pointed pencil. Repeat this process with the remaining 60 slots.

From the drawing of the side view of the harpsichord action (Figure 7), determine the position of the centerline of each row of jacks in reference to the front edge of the belly rail. Transfer these measurements from the drawing to the piece of plastic and draw two parallel lines the length of the guide, one line for each row of jacks. Center-punch the intersection of the cross lines with these two centerlines. Using a 17/64-inch drill and a drill press, carefully drill the guide holes in the Plexiglas. Be sure that the plastic is properly aligned and clamped before drilling each hole. After all of the holes have been drilled, chuck a countersink in the drill press and countersink each hole on both sides. Be careful not to enlarge the holes in the process.

Measure 1/4 inch in from the rear edge of the jack guide and draw a line the length of the piece of plastic. Locate the positions for five equally spaced screw holes along this line. Drill and countersink the holes for #8 × 1″ flathead steel wood screws. Cut a 1/2″ × 1 3/4″ piece of pine the same length as the Plexiglas to serve as a support for the jack guide. Position the jack guide on the piece of pine so that its back edge is flush with that of the support. Mark the location of the screw holes and drill pilot holes for the screws in the piece of pine. Locate four screw holes on the centerline of the face of the strip of wood. Position these holes so they will not interfere with the screws holding the jack guide to the support. Drill and countersink clearance holes for #8 × 1 1/4″ flathead steel wood screws. Join the jack guide to its support with the 1-inch screws. The jack guide will not be installed at this time.

Constructing the Soundboard

The soundboard of the harpsichord is constructed from 1/8-inch quarter-sawed spruce. When purchasing the spruce, be sure to specify the overall length needed. Also, buy at least 25 percent more total square feet than needed to allow for waste. Protect the surface of the spruce at all times, for it is soft and easily dented. Soundboards also may be ordered glued up, sawed, and sanded to size. This is considerably more expensive than gluing up one's own soundboard, but it does insure a good piece of spruce.

Begin the construction of the soundboard by making a pattern for it taken from the case rather than the plans. Make the pattern from cardboard at least one inch longer than the actual length of the soundboard to allow for trimming to an exact fit.

Cut and lay lengths of spruce over the cardboard pattern in stair-step fashion, being certain to allow extra length and width for trimming and jointing. Joint each length of spruce and trial fit them together. For this, a large, flat work surface such as a sheet of plywood will be needed. The work surface should be at least as long as the longest length of the soundboard and about six inches wider. Joint a piece of 3/4″ × 3″ wood so it is true on one edge and fasten it along the length of one side of the work surface. This board will serve as a stop against which the glued-up spruce will be clamped. Either C-clamps or nails can be used to fasten the strip of wood in place.

Prepare six or eight pairs of wedges from 3/4″ × 1 1/2″ × 5″ pieces of pine as shown in Figure 56. Make a trial clamping by laying the two longest boards on the work surface and butting them against one another and against the stop that already is in place. Clamp or nail a second stop temporarily in place about two inches away from the edge of the second piece of spruce. Space the pairs of wedges the length of the soundboard between the stop and the edge of the second piece of spruce. Gently tap one part of each wedge with a small hammer to force the two pieces of spruce together to achieve a tight joint. Do not use excessive force. Check the joint for fit and correct it if necessary. When satisfied with the fit, loosen the wedges and remove the second length of spruce. Place a four-inch-wide strip of waxpaper halfway under the first piece of spruce to prevent the soundboard from being glued to the work surface. Apply glue to the edges of the two pieces of spruce. Press the wood together, insert wedges, and apply clamping force. Place heavy weights on top of the two pieces of wood to prevent them from bowing upward. Remove excess glue with a damp sponge. Check the joint to be sure the two surfaces are flush. If not, press the raised edge down. Recheck each set of wedges for even pressure and allow the glue to set.

57. *Clamping Wedges in Use*

Succeeding lengths of spruce are glued to the preceeding pair in the same fashion, moving the temporary stop over each time. Again, be sure to put waxpaper under the joint, to check each joint, and to remove excess glue.

When the soundboard is glued, it can be turned over and excess glue can be removed from the underside of the joints. Use a steel scraper for this work rather than abrasive paper. Handle the soundboard very carefully, for it is quite fragile. Place the cardboard pattern on top of the soundboard and draw around it. Saw off the surplus wood except at the belly-rail end. A little surplus length here will prove useful in fitting. Use a fine-toothed saw to cut the spruce, since quarter-sawed spruce tends to splinter easily. Be certain to support the soundboard when sawing to prevent the wood from cracking. Clean up any ragged edges and trial fit the soundboard to the harpsichord case. Using a small plane and fine-toothed wood rasp, remove all excess wood until the soundboard fits exactly in

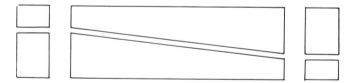

56. *Plan for Clamping Wedges*

place. At this point the position of the belly rail should be marked on the underside of the soundboard. Cut off the excess length.

Once the soundboard has been fitted to the case, the sound hole can be located and cut. The sound hole is best cut with a circle cutter such as that used on guitars. Lacking this, use a sharp knife and carefully cut around the circumference of the sound hole repeatedly, each time going a little deeper into the wood. Press a pin through the centerpoint of the sound hole so it pierces the board. Turn the soundboard over and, using the hole just pierced as a guide, redraw the sound hole, and proceed to cut around its circumference. With a little care, it is possible to cut cleanly through the spruce. Remove any roughness on the inner edges of the sound hole with a piece of sandpaper wrapped around a cylinder slightly smaller than the sound hole.

Scrape and sand the top of the soundboard so that it is level and free of any glue stains or other blemishes. Start with #2 garnet paper followed by #4 and end with #6. Use a padded sanding block and always sand with the grain. Remove all of the imperfections with the #2 grit and use finer grits for finish sanding.

Fitting the Bridge. The bridge is cut from a piece of 3/4-inch-thick hardwood free of any warp. Walnut or maple are good choices. If possible, select a board that has a grain pattern that generally follows the curve of the bridge. This will produce a stronger bridge. If a board cannot be found that is wide enough, glue extra lengths of wood to each side of a narrower board to produce the desired width.

Make a pattern of the centerline of the bridge from the working drawing by tracing it on a piece of cardboard. Extend the bridge line at each end 1 inch beyond the position of the last string. Transfer the pattern to the hardwood board and draw a second and third line 3/8 inch to either side of the centerline.

Cut the bridge out, using a fine-toothed blade in a saber saw, jig saw, or band saw. Any errors made in cutting out the bridge should fall outside the pencil lines so the width of the finished bridge will not be diminished. Handle the cut-out bridge with care, for it can crack easily in the areas where the curvature crosses the grain.

To lay out the position of the bridge pins on the bridge, fasten the two jack slides to the top of a workbench or other surface, parallel to one another, and spaced sufficiently apart to accommodate the bridge between them. Since the bridge is 3/4 inch high and the slides are only 1/2 inch high, it will be necessary to raise the slides with 1/4-inch blocks. Double-faced tape can be used to hold the blocks to the workbench and the slides to the blocks. Be sure that the slots in the two slides are in perfect alignment with one another. This is most easily accomplished by positioning the first slot in each guide the same distance in from the edge of the workbench. Also, be sure that the row of semicircular notches is toward the outside edge of the slides.

A straightedge of metal or wood will be needed. A 1/4" × 1 1/2" × 72" bar of aluminum can be found at most hardware stores and will work well. A 3/16-inch-diameter rod should be threaded for 1/2 inch of its length with a 3/16 inch × 32 die. The rod should be cut off about 1/4 inch beyond the threaded portion and a second, identical peg should be made. Drill a hole on the centerline of the aluminum bar about 4 inches in from one end and thread it with a 3/16" × 32 tap. Screw one of the pegs into this hole. Place the bar across the two jack slides, with this peg in the first slot of one of the slides. Mark the position for the second peg so it will fit in the corresponding slot in the second jack slide. Drill and tap the aluminum bar and screw the second peg in.

Saw a 6-inch length of 1/4-inch hardwood exactly 3/8 inch wide. Place the aluminum straightedge in the first slot on the treble end and place the 3/8-inch piece of wood against it where it crosses the bridge. The outside edge of this piece of wood should fall exactly on the bridge where the first treble string is to fit. Mark the position of the treble end of the bridge. Place the straightedge in the last slot on the bass end of the jack slides. The edge of the straightedge without the 3/8-inch piece of wood should fall exactly on the bridge where the last bass string is to fit. Mark the position of the bass end of the bridge. Fasten the bridge in this position with double-faced tape. Recheck the bridge position to be sure it is correctly aligned with the jack slides.

Place the straightedge once again in the first slot in the treble end, lay the 3/8-inch block of wood against it and, with the block of wood as a guide, scribe a line across the bridge with a sharp scriber or knife. Remove the block of wood and scribe a second line, using the aluminum straightedge as a guide. Move the straightedge to the second slot in both jack slides and repeat the above procedures. Continue these steps for each of the slots. Be careful to move only one slot at a time. Stop and count the slots every once in awhile to be sure the same number of moves has been made across each jack slide.

Center punch the position of each bridge pin along the centerline of the bridge. Select a drill for the size of center pin that will be used as bridge pins. The drill should be slightly smaller than the pin. Drill a vertical hole in the bridge for each bridge pin. The hole should be 1/8 inch shallower than the length of the center pin. A drill press is useful here to insure that the holes are drilled accurately.

Using a small plane and a wood rasp, shape the bridge to the cross-section shown in Figure 3. Be certain that the peak falls in back of the bridge pin line so when the strings cross the bridge a metal-to-metal contact will be made. A wood-to-metal contact would dampen the sound. Cut off each end of the bridge at a slight angle 3/8 inch beyond the last bridge-pin hole. Sand the bridge on all sides except the bottom. Use an unpadded sanding block on the top edges to preserve the sharpness of the peak.

Locate and mark the exact position of the bridge on the soundboard. Place the bridge in this position and trial-clamp it. There are two ways this clamping can be done. First, if the workshop ceiling above the work surface is solid and can be marked up, thin laths of wood about 1/4 to 3/8 inch thick and 3/4 to 1 inch wide and an inch or so longer than the distance between the top of the bridge and the ceiling can be sprung into place along the length of the bridge. These are called "go bars" and provide a very practical way for clamping the bridge to the soundboard. If go bars cannot be used, the second method is to use a series of weights (books, bricks, cans of nails) along the length of the bridge to provide the necessary pressure. When satisfied with the clamping arrangement, apply glue to both the bridge and the soundboard and clamp them together. Remove excess glue and allow the glue to set.

Installing the Cutoff Bar and Ribs. The cutoff bar and ribs (Figure 58) are glued to the underside of the soundboard after the bridge has been glued into place. Turn the soundboard upside down on the work surface and support it with 3/4-inch boards so it will lie level where the cutoff bar and ribs are to be placed. Mark the position of the cutoff bar and ribs on the soundboard. Prepare the cutoff bar from 1/2″ × 1 3/4″ clear spruce with the grain running vertically. Glue the cutoff bar to the soundboard, using the same procedures as were used with the bridge. Remove any excess glue. Prepare the ribs to the same general profile as the cutoff bar, using 1/4″ × 1″ clear spruce. Glue them in place in the same way. Using a sharp chisel,

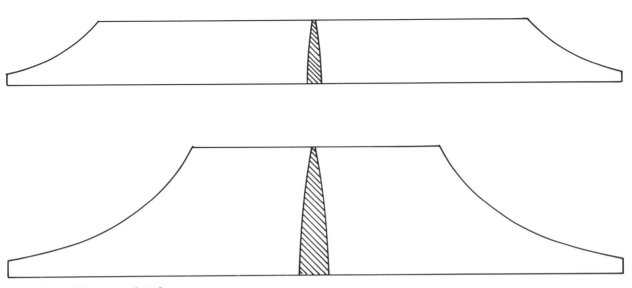

58. *Cutoff Bar and Ribs*

59. *Go Bars Clamping Cutoff Bar to Sound Board*

shape the ends of the cutoff bar and ribs in a shallow curve as shown in Figure 58.

Installing the Soundboard. Check the fit of the finished soundboard in the harpsichord case to be sure that neither the ribs nor the cutoff bar prevent the soundboard from resting firmly on the belly rail and liner. Clean all chips and dust out of the harpsichord case with a vacuum cleaner. If you desire, the inside of the soundbox can be signed and dated. Coat the edges of the soundboard, belly rail, and liner with glue. Slide the soundboard into position and clamp it by driving 1/2-inch brads through the soundboard into the liner and belly rail. Remove all excess glue. When the glue has set, countersink the brads below the surface of the wood and fill the holes with crack filler. When hardened, sand off any excess crack filler level with the surface of the soundboard.

Fitting the Hitch-Pin Rail and Soundboard Molding. At their extreme end, the strings of the harpsichord are attached to hitch pins embedded in the hitch-pin rail. The strings run from the hitch pins across the bridge on the soundboard, across the nut on the wrest plank, and terminate at the tuning pins, which are embedded in the wrest plank. The hitch-pin rail is cut from hardwood, rectangular in cross-section, measuring 1/2″ × 1″ with the upper front edge slightly rounded.

Fit the hitch-pin rail as closely as possible to the bent side and tail of the harpsichord case. Miter the joints between the two sections of the hitch-pin rail. Fit the soundboard molding along the short side and the spine in the same way.

Locate the positions of the hitch pins on the hitch-pin rail from the harpsichord plans and drill the holes for the pins with a 1/16-inch drill bit. Sand the hitch-pin rail and soundboard molding. Trial-clamp the hitch-pin rail, using go bars and deep-throated clamps to hold the rail down against

the soundboard and tightly against the sides of the case. When satisfied with the clamping arrangement, remove the hitch-pin rail and apply glue to it and to the surface of the soundboard where it will fit. Put the hitch-pin rail in place and draw it snugly against the soundboard and the sides of the case. Remove any excess glue. Apply the soundboard molding in the same way. Do not put the hitch pins in until after the soundboard and the bridge have been varnished.

Fitting the Wrest Plank

Before the wrest plank may be fitted to the harpsichord case, the wrest-plank blocks must be cut out and glued in place. The wrest-plank blocks are made from 1 1/2-inch-thick clear, hard maple or similar dense hardwood cut to the shape and measurements given in Figure 60.

Clear the corners of the harpsichord case between the side, bottom, and belly rail of any dust or chips so that the wrest-plank blocks will fit in the proper position with the projecting 1 1/2-inch-wide end butting against the belly rail. Temporarily clamp each wrest-plank block against the side, being sure that it presses firmly against the belly rail and the bottom of the case. Drill five clearance holes for #6 × 1 1/4″ flathead steel wood screws through the sides of the case into each wrest-plank block. Trial-drive each screw into position. A dab of wax applied to the threads of the screws will make screwing them into the hardwood easier. Check to be sure the heads of the screws are countersunk below the surface of the sides. Do not glue the blocks in at this time in case any adjustments must be made to them during the fitting of the wrest plank.

The wrest plank is cut from a piece of clear, hard maple or similar dense hardwood 1 1/2 inch thick, 9 inches wide, and as long as the inner width of the harpsichord case measured at the top edge of the belly rail.

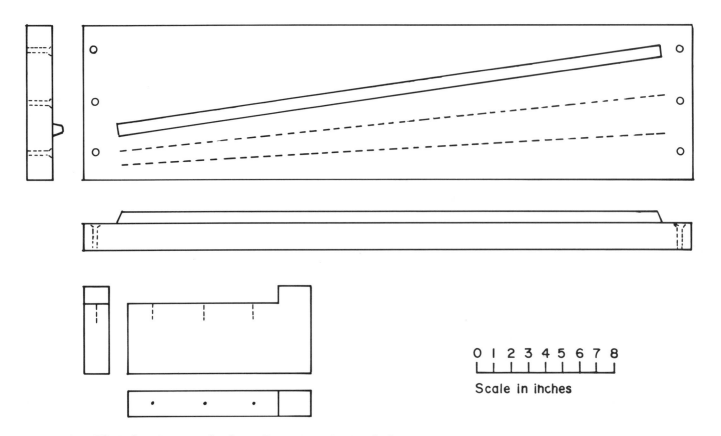

60. Plan for Wrest Plank and Wrest Plank Blocks

Place the wrest plank into position so it rests in the notches in the wrest-plank blocks. Check to be sure it makes a close-fitting joint where it rests against the blocks. This is essential, because all of the strain placed on the wrest plank by the tension of the strings must be resisted by these two joints. Make any adjustments necessary to the wrest plank or the blocks to insure the accuracy of the fit. Temporarily clamp the wrest plank in position, being sure it fits snugly against the gap projections on the wrest-plank blocks. Incidentally, these projections will be 1/2 inch lower than the top edge of the wrest plank to form a recess for the jack slides. Drill clearance holes through each end of the wrest plank and pilot holes into the wrest-plank blocks for three #10 × 3″ flathead steel wood screws. Space the holes 3 inches apart and 3/4 inch in from the ends. Lubricate each screw with wax and drive it in with a brace fitted with a screwdriver bit.

If the holes seem too tight and there is danger of the screws shearing, remove the screws and enlarge the pilot holes slightly. When everything is fitted, remove the wrest plank and wrest-plank blocks from the harpsichord case. Apply glue to the blocks and the sides and bottom of the case, and clamp the blocks into position with the screws. Remove all excess glue, especially in the notch where the wrest plank fits. Do not glue the wrest plank in at this time.

Making the Nut. To make the nut, cut a piece of 3/4″ × 3/4″ hardwood of the same kind as used for the bridge. It should be long enough to extend 3/4 inch beyond the last bridge pin at each end. Draw a centerline along the length of one side of the nut. Again using the jack slides as gauges, lay out and center punch the location of each bridge pin in the same manner as was done on the bridge. Be sure to hold the bridge at the same angle to the jack slides as it will be in the finished instrument. Drill the holes for the bridge pins with a 1/16-inch drill bit. Shape the drilled nut to the same cross-section as the bridge and cut off the ends at an angle 3/8 inch beyond the last bridge-pin hole.

Put the wrest plank in its proper position in the harpsichord case and hold it in place with a single screw at each end. Referring to the plans and to the bridge on the soundboard, locate the exact position of the nut on the wrest plank and glue the nut in position. Be certain that the nut is correctly located in relationship to the bridge and that the bridge-pin holes at each end of the nut are the same distance from the sides of the case as those on the bridge to insure that the strings will lie parallel to the case and to each other.

Drilling the Tuning-Pin Holes. Using measurements taken from the plans, draw the two lines along the length of the wrest plank on which the centers of the tuning pins will be located. The position of each tuning pin on these lines must be determined accurately so the strings passing to the second row of tuning pins do not bind against or interfere with the first row of tuning pins. The tuning pin for the first bridge pin on the treble end should go to the first row of tuning pins, the second pin to the second row, and repeat. Each string will pass by the left side of the bridge pin on the nut, make a slight angle to the right and

61. *Scribing the Nut*

downward, and wrap around the tuning pin in a clockwise fashion when viewed from above as shown in Figure 19. Use an adjustable bevel to determine the best angle and then center punch the location of each tuning pin.

Using a scrap block of the wood stock used for the wrest plank, drill a series of test holes in varying diameters smaller than the diameter of the tuning pins. Drive a tuning pin into each hole and test the fit with the tuning wrench. The tuning pin should turn smoothly under firm pressure. If the tuning pin turns too freely, the hole is too large; if the tuning pin turns too hard and with a jerky motion, the hole is too small. Once the drill of the proper size has been selected, the holes for the tuning pins can be drilled in the wrest plank. The use of a drill press will help to insure accuracy in drilling these holes. Do not install the tuning pins at this time.

Constructing the Harp Stop. The harp stop (Figure 20) is made from a piece of 1/2" × 3/4" × 33 3/4" hardwood. Once again, the jack slides are used to mark the spacing on the harp batten in the same manner as was used for the nut. Begin 1 1/2 inches in from the treble end of the harp batten and scribe one line on the batten for each slot on the jack slide.

Turn the batten on its side and with a square transfer the lines on the top of the batten to the rear edge. Next draw a line 1/4 inch in from the edge on both the top and bottom of the batten.

Clamp the batten in a vise and, using a small back saw with a .015-inch kerf, saw along each line at the angle drawn until the saw cut meets the line drawn 1/4 inch in from the edge. Check the size of the saw kerf by measuring the width of the teeth with a micrometer or by making a trial cut in a scrap of hardwood. A strip of 26 gauge (.016-inch) brass driven into the slot with a small hammer should fit tightly and resist efforts to pull it out of the slot.

After the slots in the batten have been sawed, remove the batten from the vise and locate on it the position of the slots for the hold-down screws. One slot should be at the middle and the other two should be 2 inches in from each end. The slots should be 3/16 inch wide and 3/4 inch long, centered 1/4 inch in from the front edge. Drill a 3/16-inch hole at each end of the slot and cut out the intervening wood with a jig saw or coping saw. File the edges of the slot smooth, being careful not to widen the slots excessively. Round off all the top edges with 2/0, 4/0, 6/0, and then 8/0 garnet paper.

The metal tabs for the harp batten are cut from 1/4-inch wide, 26-gauge brass strips. Sixty-one pieces 7/8 inch long are required. After the tabs have been cut, round off the corners and remove any sharp edges with a smooth-cut file.

Clamp the batten to the workbench so the slotted edge is up and the front of the batten faces away from the viewer. Insert one of the brass tabs into the first slot so its edge is even with the bottom edge of the batten. Drive it into the slot with light taps of a small hammer. If a tab fits too loosely, use a center punch and make a small dimple with it about 1/4 inch in from the end of the tab. The dimple should be visible on the back side; it will serve to wedge the tab in the slot.

When all of the tabs have been fitted to the batten strip, file the side and back of the batten to remove any protruding tab edges. Place the harp stop on the wrest plank parallel to, but about 1/16 inch in front of, the nut. Position the harp stop so the tabs are centered in the space between each pair of strings. Mark the wrest plank at the midpoint of each hold-down slot and drill a pilot hole for a #6 × 1" roundhead brass wood screw. Trial-fit the harp stop by fastening it down with three screws. Place a small flat brass washer under each screw head before inserting them in the slot. Drive them down until they hold the harp stop tightly, then back them off just enough to allow the harp stop to slide freely.

Remove the harp stop from the wrest plank and give it two coats of polyurethane varnish. When the varnish has dried, cut 1/4-inch squares of 1/8-inch-thick adhesive-backed urethane foam (the type used for weatherstripping around doors and windows). Remove the paper backing from each foam square and adhere it to the upper end on the bass side of each metal tab. If desired, small blocks of felt can be substituted for the urethane foam. Because of the nonporous nature of metal, it will be necessary to use a rubber cement or modeler's cement to attach the felt to the metal tabs.

Building the Keyboard

The construction of the keyboard begins with building the key frame. The base of the key frame is made from 1/2-inch plywood. It should measure 16 3/4 inches wide and 32 3/8 inches long. The grain in the uppermost layer of the plywood should run lengthwise to add rigidity to the frame. Cut the balance rail from 3/4-inch-thick hardwood (maple or walnut), 2 1/2 inches wide and 32 3/8 inches long. Do not chamfer the edges at this time. Cut the back rail from 5/8-inch-thick hardwood, 3 inches wide and 32 3/8 inches long. Cut the front rail from 1/4-inch hardwood, 2 3/4 inches wide and 32 3/8 inches long. From the plans, locate the position of each rail on the base and glue them into place. Go bars may be substituted for deep-throated clamps for clamping the balance rail if the latter clamps are not available.

The keyboard is cut from a glued-up blank of 3/4-inch-thick clear, white pine or basswood. Its finished dimensions are 16 inches wide by 32 1/4 inches long. However, it should be made slightly oversize in both width and length, and then trimmed accurately to the finished size after gluing. Traditionally, the keyboard is glued up from 6 1/4-inches-wide lengths of wood, with the glue joint located so it falls either between the keys B and C, or E and F. In this way the glue joint is sawed out in the process of cutting out the keys. Therefore, prepare five lengths of wood 6 1/4 inches wide and 17 inches long. Prepare a sixth piece 1 inch wide and 17 inches long. Joint the pieces accurately so when they are glued together they will present an even surface. Glue and clamp the pieces together using bar clamps or the wedge-clamping arrangement used to glue up the soundboard.

When the glue has set, remove the keyboard blank from the clamps and joint one long edge square to the glue joints. Cut and joint the opposite long edge so the keyboard blank measures exactly 16 inches wide. Trim the end with the 1-inch piece so the finished length of the keyboard blank measures exactly 32 1/8 inches long.

Following the steps given in the previous section for drawing the keyboard, lay out the keys on the keyboard blank. Be sure that the line between keys E and F falls on the glue line. Center punch the position for the balance-rail pins and the guide pins. Be sure they are located on the centerline of each key lever. Draw lines across the keyboard blank 1/4 inch on each side of the two rows of balance-rail pins and the row of guide pins. These lines will be used as guides for cutting out the slots for these pins. Draw a diagonal line starting slightly above the balance-rail pin on FF and ending slightly below the guide pin on f³. Beginning at the left, number each key with a pencil. The numbers and the diagonal line will help to locate the position of each key after it is sawed.

Place a scrap piece of 3/4-inch-thick wood on the key frame just in front of the back rail. Position the keyboard blank on top of the key frame so the front edge of the keyboard blank is in 1/4 inch from the front edge of the key frame and the ends of the blank are in 1/8 inch from each end of the key frame. Clamp the assembly together, checking for accuracy of alignment between the keyboard blank and the key frame. Use pads when clamping to avoid marring the soft wood of the keys. Do not place the clamps where the balance-rail pin or guide-pin holes will be drilled. If desirable, clamps can be placed along the front edge of the assembly by using a 1/2-inch piece of wood as a filler strip on top of the front rail.

Select a drill bit approximately .005 inch smaller in diameter than the diameter of the balance rail and guide pins. Thus, if the pin is .146 inch in diameter (a standard size) use a #27 (.144 inch) or a #28 (.141 inch) drill bit. Test the fit of the drill bit by drilling a hole in a piece of hardwood and hammering in a sample pin. The fit should be tight but not so tight that the wood could be split. Use the drill bit that gives the best fit.

Place the keyboard and key-frame assembly on the table of a drill press and adjust the depth stop on the drill press so that the hole for the balance-rail pin will be 1 3/4 inches deep (assuming the length of the pin to be 2 inches). This will allow the balance-rail pin to stand 1/4 inch above the top surface of the key. Drill a hole for each balance-rail pin in the precise position indicated on the key blank. When this has been completed, readjust the depth stop so the hole for the guide pin will be only 1 1/2 inches deep. This will allow the guide pin to stand 1/2 inch above the top surface of the key. Accurately align and drill the holes for the guide pins. When drilling, it may be necessary to remove clamps at one end of the assembly so the key-frame base can sit level on the drill press table. When doing this, be sure that at least three other clamps are in position so the keyboard will not shift out of alignment.

When the drilling has been completed, unclamp the assembly and remove the keyboard blank from the key frame. Use a plane to chamfer both edges of the balance rail as shown in Figure 3. Cut out the key slip (the piece of trim fastened to the front edge of the key frame) from a piece of hardwood of the same type used for the harpsichord case. Sand the key frame, then dust it and vacuum any chips from the balance rail and guide-pin holes. Use a small-diameter nail to check each hole for freedom from chips and proper depth. Re-drill any shallow holes. Drive the balance rail and guide pins into their respective holes with a hammer. A small block of wood cut to the right height can be used to insure that each pin is driven in the proper distance. Check that each pin stands vertical to the base.

Cut a 32-inch length of 1 1/2-inch-wide, medium-thick (.185 inch) key cloth and glue it into position on the back rail just behind the guide pins. Cut a 32-inch length of 2 3/4-inch-wide key cloth of the same thickness and glue it into position on the front rail. Place a thin (.065-inch) balance rail punching over every balance-rail pin.

Using a band saw or jig saw with a fine-toothed blade, saw the keyboard blank apart along the lines between E and F. Use great care to follow the lines exactly so there will not be large gaps between the finished sides of the keys. Next, saw apart the resultant octave-wide boards along the line between B and C. To separate the natural keys from the accidental keys, begin by sawing along the line between the heads of the two natural keys until the front end of the accidental key is reached (see Figure 62). Turn the key blank around 180 degrees and cut along the line between the natural key and the accidental key until the front end of the accidental key is reached (see Figure 63). Using a coping saw or jig saw with a fine-toothed blade, insert the blade along the line sawed at the head of the key, turn it 90 degrees and cut across the end of the accidental key (see figure 64). This will release the natural key from the accidental key. To speed up the cutting out of the keys, make all the lengthwise saw cuts for the natural-key heads first and then separate the

62. *Sawing the Head Ends of the Keys*

63. *Sawing the Tail Ends of the Keys*

64. *Separating the Keys*

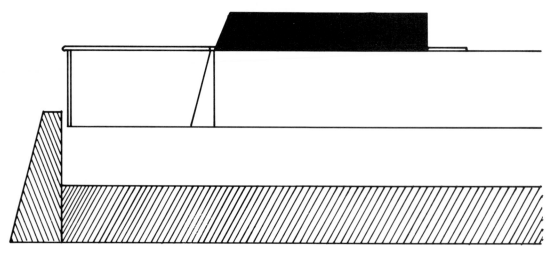

65. *Detail Showing Key Clearance*

naturals from the accidentals. After all of the keys have been sawed apart, a small wedge of wood should be removed from each of the natural keys as shown in Figure 65. Use a dovetail saw to cut across the grain and a sharp 3/4-inch-wide chisel to remove the waste material. The purpose of removing this wedge of wood is to prevent the end of the accidental key from binding against the natural key when it is depressed.

The slots for the balance-rail pins and the guide pins are cut with chisels. For this, both a 3/8-inch-wide and 1/8-inch-wide straight woodcarver's chisels will be needed. These chisels have thin blades, less than 1/8 inch in thickness, in comparison to the thick blade of the butt chisels used by carpenters and cabinetmakers. The chisels must be kept extremely sharp at all times so the walls of the slots in the key levers can be cut cleanly, free of ragged edges. Several practice cuts should be made in scrap pieces of pine before tackling the key slots themselves, as the slots must be cut very accurately. If they are cut too wide, the keys will wobble and rattle on the pins; if cut too narrow, the keys will bind. The slots should be 3/8 inch long (3/16 inch on either side of the centerlines of the holes drilled for the pins). The slots should be just slightly wider (a few thousandths of an inch) than the pins themselves so the key levers will ride freely on the pins. The slots for the balance rail should be cut to within 1/8 inch of the bottom of the key lever. The slots for the guide pins are cut completely through the key.

With a pencil, draw a line on both sides of the balance-rail pin and the guide-pin holes. The lines should be parallel to the centerline of the key and should connect with the two lines previously drawn in front and behind each pin hole to produce a rectangle 3/8 inch long and 1/8 inch wide.

Place the key in a vise or clamp it to the top of a workbench. Be careful not to crush or dent the key with too much pressure while clamping. If necessary use clamp pads. Using the 3/8-inch chisel, with the flat side of the blade facing outward, make a shallow cut along each 3/8-inch line. With the 1/8-inch chisel, make similar cuts at each end of the slot. Remove the waste wood by cutting from the pin hole toward each end with the small chisel. Repeat the entire process, each time making the slot deeper. A line made with a marker on the blade of one of the chisels can be used as a depth gauge to determine when the proper depth for the balance-rail pin slot has been reached. In cutting the guide-pin slot, the key can be turned over and the slot cut from the bottom after cutting halfway down from the top. Clean all rough fibers of wood from each slot when the cutting is finished. Use a spare balance-rail pin to check the width of the slot from time to time. The pin should slide easily along the length of the slot.

At this stage, the hole in the key for the balance-rail pin will be too tight to slide over the pin. Therefore, it should be enlarged slightly. If desired, the hole on the bottom of the key can be countersunk slightly. The hole can be enlarged by reaming it with a narrow reamer, by filing it with a small rattail file, or by inserting the shaft of an awl into the hole and rocking it back and forth, simultaneously pressing it inward until the wood is compressed just enough to allow the pin to slide into the hole. Check the fit by placing the key lever in its proper position on the key frame. Do not attempt to fit it in any other position, because variations in drilling will usually be sufficient to prevent the key from fitting any set of pins except its own. Place a small weight on the back end of the key and press down on the front. The key should move up and down smoothly, without wobbling or binding. If the key binds, determine where it is binding and remove a thin layer of wood from that slot. Re-check the fit of the key lever on the key frame. If the key wobbles on the pin, the area where the slot is too wide will have to be built up. Glue a thin layer of wood into place against the side of the slot that is too wide. When the glue has set, carefully shave the shim down with a sharp chisel until the key fits the pin correctly.

As the keys are fitted to the key frame, check to see that each key stands square to its neighbor. Straighten up the key pins as necessary with a mallet and a small block of wood. Do not use pliers or any tool that would scratch the surface of the pin. Such scratches may cause the key to bind or to be noisy.

When all the keys have been fitted to the key frame, they can be removed and the key coverings can be applied. This means applying a layer of hardwood to the fronts and tops of the natural keys and gluing combs to the tops of the accidental keys.

Two contrasting hardwoods should be selected, such as rosewood for the naturals and ebony for the accidentals. Begin by cutting out the blanks for the accidental combs from 1/2-inch stock to the proportions given in Figure 66. The easiest way to do this is to cut lengths of wood to the cross-section shown

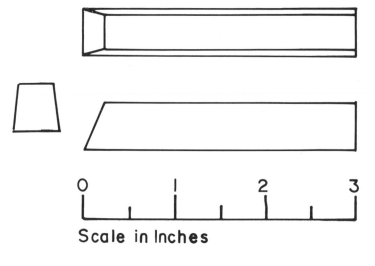

Scale in Inches

66. *Plan for the Key Combs*

and then to cut off the individual combs to the proper length. Cut the front end of the comb to the angle shown and then plane and sand each comb to remove all saw marks. Save the finish-sanding of the combs until after they have been glued to the key levers.

Glue and clamp the combs to the key levers with spring clamps or weights. Be sure that they are accurately positioned by aligning the tail of the comb with the line drawn on the key lever in the layout. When the glue has dried, unclamp the keys, remove all excess glue, and clean up the sides of the key lever. Use a small plane to remove saw marks, and finish sand the combs with 4/0 and then 6/0 garnet paper. When completed, place each key in its proper position on the key frame.

Cut out 1″ × 5 1/4″ rectangular blanks for the natural key covers from 3/32-inch-thick hardwood. Do not use a standard veneer, since it lacks sufficient thickness to be finished properly. Cut out the key front blanks 1″ × 3/4″ from the same hardwood. First glue the key fronts to the ends of the natural key levers, using three-way edging clamps or weights. When the glue has set, trim each key front flush and square to the key body. (An alternate way to apply the key fronts is to glue a length of the hardwood to the front of the keyboard blank before the keys are cut apart. Use bar clamps to hold the strip in position while the glue sets. Trim the strip flush and square to the edges and ends of the keyboard blank. As each key is cut from the blank it already will have its key front glued in place. If this method is used, the final width of the keyboard still must be held to 16 inches regardless of the thickness or form of this edging strip.)

Next, glue the key coverings into place using spring clamps or weights to hold them while the glue sets. Align the key coverings so their rear edges fall exactly on the same line as the tails of the accidental combs. After the glue has set, unclamp the keys and trim the sides of the key coverings flush with the sides of the key levers. A saw, chisel, and file are used to cut away the indented portion of the key cover. Cut the front of the key covering back to within 1/16 inch of the key front to provide a slight overhang. Finish-sand the key covers and key fronts, starting with 2/0 and ending with 6/0 garnet paper. Place each key in its proper position on the key frame as it is completed and check its fit with adjacent keys. Each key should be level and show the same amount of space on both sides between it and the other keys. Check for binding and remove any excess material cautiously to avoid creating an excessive gap between the keys. This is especially important at the front ends of the keys if they are to present a uniform appearance.

Once the keys have been covered, they are weighted to give the proper touch when played. The easiest weights to use for this purpose are called "Jiffy key leads" and are secured to the bottom of the key lever with two screws. The objective in weighting the key is to balance the key lever in relation to its pivot point on the balance rail. Then, when the jacks rest on the far end of the key, they will be the only weight added to the key, thereby providing a very light touch. A heavier touch, if desired, can be achieved by moving the key weights somewhat farther toward the tail of the key lever.

Tape a balance-rail pin or similar round rod to the workbench top to serve as a balance point. Place the first key on this rod so the hole for the balance-rail pin is exactly on top of the rod (Figure 67). Place a Jiffy key lead with its two screws on top of the rear of the key lever. Move the lead back and forth on the key lever until the key just balances. (If a heavier touch is desired, place a penny on the front end of the key during the balancing process.) Mark the position of the lead on the side of the key. Turn the key over and transfer the mark from the side to the bottom of the key lever. Place the lead in position and mark the location of the screws. Drill small pilot holes in the key lever and fasten the lead in position with the two screws. Replace the key on the key frame and repeat the procedure for the remaining keys.

Cut a 1 1/2-inch length of 1/2 inch wide by .065 inch thick bushing cloth and glue it to the top of the tail end of each key lever. The end pins of the jacks will rest on this cloth, and thus the sound of the jacks will be dampened as they drop back down on the keys after being played.

Place the completed key frame with keys into position in the harpsichord case. Line up the keys so the spaces between the lowest bass string (FF) and the highest treble strings (f^3) are exactly centered over their respective keys on the keyboard. The accuracy of this alignment is essential to the action of

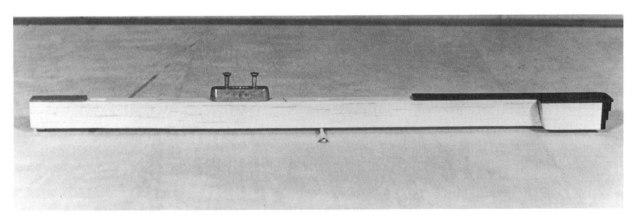

67. *Balancing the Keys*

the harpsichord. To aid in the alignment, temporarily insert bridge pins in the bridge and nut, and run a strong piece of thread around them to represent the strings. Be sure that the thread passes on the bass side of each pin, since considerable error will be encountered if it passes on the wrong side. Use a square to transfer the position of the strings to the edge of the belly rail facing the gap. Find the mid-point of each space and adjust the position of the keyboard to line up this mid-point with the centerline of the related key lever.

Once the position of the key frame has been ascertained, screw holes to hold the key frame in position can be drilled and countersunk in the bottom of the harpsichord case. Four #10 × 1 1/4″ flathead steel wood screws should be used. Space the screws so they go through the two key-frame runners attached to the inside of the case bottom and into the piece of plywood that forms the base of the key frame.

Once the position of the keyboard within the harpsichord case has been determined, the end blocks may be cut and fitted into place. The end blocks serve to fill the space between the last key on each end of the keyboard and the sides of the harpsichord case. The end blocks should be cut out of the same type of hardwood that is used to veneer the case. They should be cut so they fit snugly between the lock-board batten and the wrest-plank blocks. The end blocks should provide 1/8 inch clearance between them and the sides of the keys. They should be 1/8 inch higher than the tops of the playing surface of the natural keys. When fitted, sand the end blocks with 2/0, 4/0, and then 6/0 garnet paper; apply glue and clamp them into position in the harpsichord case.

Finally the key slip can be cut from hardwood to the shape shown in Figure 7. Glue the key slip to the key frame so it extends across the width of the case in front of the end blocks.

Constructing the Nameboard

The nameboard (Figure 7) is constructed from 1/2-inch plywood. It should be long enough to fit between the two sides and wide enough to reach from 1/8 inch above the key levers to 1/2 inch above the jack rail. The bracket by which the nameboard is secured to the wrest plank should be made from 1/2″ × 1″ hardwood. Veneer is applied to all surfaces of the nameboard in the same manner as the case was veneered. The holes for the stop mechanism are drilled with a 3/8-inch bit. Three #8 × 1 1/4″ roundhead brass wood screws are used to fasten the nameboard to the wrest plank. After the finish has been applied to the nameboard, a piece of 1/2-inch-wide nameboard felt should be glued to its lower edge to keep dust from the interior of the instrument.

Constructing the Jack Rail and Music Desk

The jack rail (Figure 7) is made from 1/2-inch plywood with a 1/2″ × 3/4″ hardwood trim glued to its front edge and 1/8-inch hardwood protective strips glued to the remaining three edges. The jack rail is veneered top and bottom as explained earlier.

The jack rail is secured in the harpsichord with heavy-duty magnetic catches. The catches are screwed to the sides of the harpsichord case, and the metal strike plates are attached to the underside of the jack rail. Since the jack rail serves to stop the upward motion of the jacks and also controls the key dip, it is important that the magnetic catches are accurately located. The correct height is determined by measuring the distance the jacks extend above the wrest plank when the keys are at rest. To this measurement is added 5/16 to 3/8 inch for the key dip and 1/4 inch for the thickness of the jack-rail cloth. This combined measurement represents the distance between the underside of the jack rail

68. Music Desk Installation

and the top of the wrest plank. The catches should be installed at this height.

After the final finish has been applied to the jack rail, a piece of 1/4″ × 2″ felt is glued in position on the underside with Titebond or a similar adhesive.

Making the Music Desk. The music desk is cut from 1/2-inch plywood, 8 inches wide and 16 inches long. It is veneered on all sides and

edges. The music desk hinges are fastened to the jack rail with small bolts and to the music desk itself with small flathead screws. Both the bolts and screws are furnished with the hinges. The music desk support (Figure 68) is screwed to the jack rail, and the small staple is fastened to the back of the music desk to hold the desk at an angle of about 20 degrees from the vertical.

Constructing the Lid

The outline of the harpsichord lid is obtained by placing a sheet of 1/2-inch plywood on top of the case and aligning one edge of the plywood with the outside edge of the spine. The other outside edges of the case are traced on the plywood with a pencil. Remove the sheet of plywood from the harpsichord and mark the dividing line between the first and second panels. Saw the lid out, following the lines very carefully. Cut strips of 1/4" × 1/2" hardwood and fit them to the edges of the second panel, using mitered joints at the corners. Clamp the panel to a flat surface when gluing these strips in place to prevent accidental warping or bowing. Either three-way edging clamps or small brads can be used to hold the strips in position until the glue sets. If brads are used, they should be countersunk and the holes filled with a matching plastic wood during the finishing operation.

Once the hardwood edgings have been applied to the second panel, the first panel can be fitted to it. Begin by gluing a 1/4" × 1/2" strip of hardwood to the back edge of the first panel. Place the second panel on top of the harpsichord so it extends 1/4 inch on the sides and at the tail. Slide the first panel snugly into place against the main part of the lid and mark the location of the apex of the case where the key cover begins. Subtract 1/2 inch from this measurement and cut the first panel to this width. Glue a 1/2" × 3/4" strip of hardwood to the front edge of the first panel and a 1/4" × 1/2" strip to both ends. Joint the front edge of the first panel to the angle shown in Figure 7.

The keyboard cover is constructed from two pieces of 1/2-inch plywood cut to the dimensions given. Make the joint as shown and glue the two pieces together. When the glue has set, cut a strip of 1/2" × 3/4" hardwood and glue it to the rear edge of the keyboard cover. Joint the edge of this piece of hardwood so its angle matches that on the first panel. Using mitered joints, cut and glue strips of 1/4" × 1/2" hardwood around the remaining three edges. When this step is complete, check the fit of all three parts of the lid. There should be 1/4 inch of overhang all the way around, except the lower edge of the keyboard cover should rest evenly on the lock board. Make any adjustment necessary to secure a good fit of the lid to the case.

Following the procedures outlined earlier, apply veneer to both surfaces of the first panel, second panel, and keyboard cover. Trim the veneer flush with the edges and sand lightly to remove any splinters and traces of cement.

The three parts of the lid assembly are fastened to one another and to the harpsichord case with hinges. The nine hinges used can be as plain or as fancy as desired, but, in any case, the three hinges joining the lid assembly to the spine should be furnished with loose pins to facilitate removing the lid assembly from the harpsichord case. Also, note that the hinges that hold the lid to the spine are taken apart and reassembled so the finished surface of one leaf of each hinge faces the unfinished surface of the other leaf of the hinge. This allows one leaf of the hinge to be screwed to the outside surface of the harpsichord spine and the other leaf of the hinge to the underside surface of the lid. Use a depth gauge when drilling pilot holes for the hinge screws to avoid piercing the side of the case or the lid opposite the hinge.

The lid support is constructed from hardwood to the dimensions given in Figure 69. It tapers from a rectangular to a circular cross-section. The lid support is fastened to the side of the case with a small hinge as shown in Figure 70. A #8 × 1 1/2 inch flathead brass wood screw is screwed into the soundboard molding directly beneath the lid support. This screw may be turned in or out so that it will hold the lid support just above the

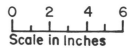

Scale in Inches

69. *Plan for Lid Support*

70. **Lid Support Installation**

71. *Lid Support Socket*

strings when the lid is closed. A 1 1/2-inch-diameter ring should be cut from 1/4-inch-thick hardwood and glued to the underside of the lid to serve as a socket for the lid support (see Figure 71). The socket should be so located as to hold the lid open at an angle of approximately 45 degrees.

When all parts of the lid assembly and lid support have been constructed and fitted, they should be carefully sanded in preparation for applying the finish.

Finishing the Case

Once all of the parts of the harpsichord have been completed, the instrument is ready to be finished and assembled. As a general rule, all of the wooden parts are sanded and finished before the hardware is installed.

If it has not been done, begin by gluing the wrest plank in place, using the three screws at each end to provide clamping pressure. Sand all of the wooden parts of the instrument, using progressively finer grits of abrasive paper. Begin with 2/0 and finish with 8/0 garnet paper. Be sure to brush or wipe away all sanding dust when changing from one grit to another. A vacuum cleaner with a crevice tool is useful for cleaning dust and dirt from the corners and the tuning-pin and bridge-pin holes. When the sanding has been completed, inspect each surface thoroughly for scratches or stains. Re-sand where necessary.

Apply flat polyurethane varnish to the soundboard and to the top and edges of the wrest plank, following the manufacturer's directions. Do not varnish the bridge or nut. The bottom of the harpsichord case should be either varnished or painted with a flat black or brown enamel. Various types of finishes can be applied to the hardwood parts of the instrument, depending upon the builder's preference in such matters. A durable and easily applied non-commercial finish, known as oil-and-varnish finish, can be mixed from spar varnish (the best that can be afforded), boiled linseed oil, and turpentine. Directions for mixing and applying this finish follow.

Mix a sealer coat, consisting of one-part spar varnish to one-part turpentine. With a rag, apply a generous coat of this sealer to the bare wood, coating only an area of two or three square feet at a time. Allow the sealer to soak into the wood for several minutes and then wipe away with a lint-free cloth all traces of the sealer from the surface of the wood. Allow the sealer coat to dry for at least 24 hours and then sand lightly with 8/0 abrasive paper. Wipe off all sanding dust with a tack rag.

Mix one-part spar varnish with one-part boiled linseed oil and two-parts turpentine. Apply this mixture generously with a rag to the surface of the wood, rubbing it into the wood for several minutes. Stop rubbing before the surface becomes tacky, and wipe away with a lint-free cloth all traces of the finishing material from the surface. Let the finish dry for at least 48 hours or until the smell of turpentine disappears. Rub the dry surface with 00 steel wool, dust thoroughly with a tack rag, and repeat the above procedures until at least three coats of the oil-varnish mixture have been applied. Give the surface of the wood a final rub with steel wool, apply a good grade of paste wax, and buff to a satiny sheen with a soft cloth or lamb's wool pad.

A word of caution concerning this finish. The rags used to wipe on and wipe off the oil and varnish mixture must be stored in an airtight metal container to prevent a fire from spontaneous combustion. As an alternative, the rags can be washed thoroughly in a strong, hot detergent solution, rinsed well, and hung up to dry.

When the finish has been applied to all of the wooden parts, the harpsichord can be mounted on its stand and the keyboard, nameboard, lid support, and jack rail can be installed. The various parts of the lid assembly can be hinged together and then hinged to the spine of the harpsichord case. When this has been completed, remove the hinge pins at the spine, fold the lid assembly back upon itself, lift the lid from the harpsichord and set it aside until the instrument has been assembled, adjusted, and tuned.

Constructing the Jacks

For reasons discussed previously, plastic is recommended for the jack bodies. Two commonly used plastics are Delrin (acetal resin) and Plexiglas (acrylic resin). Both are easily machined using ordinary woodworking tools and techniques. Of the two, Delrin probably is the best choice for jack bodies. It is stable over a wide range of temperatures and humidity, tough and resilient, and possesses a low coefficient of friction. The major drawback to the use of Delrin is its cost—it is about five times as expensive as Plexiglas.

Plexiglas, although not possessing all of the qualities of Delrin, is an economical and practical alternative material for jack bodies. The major drawback to the use of Plexiglas is its comparative brittleness and low melting point. These two qualities can cause problems in machining. For example, when drilling thin sections, a feed rate that is too fast may cause the Plexiglas to crack. When sawing, a feed rate that is too fast may cause the plastic to melt and produce ragged rather than smooth cut edges. Also, a feed rate that is too fast when tapping can cause the tap to be seized by the plastic. This leads to tap breakage and spoiled parts. However, all of these machining problems can be overcome simply by using a slower rate of feed and sharp cutting tools. Regardless of the materials chosen for the jack bodies, the instructions that follow are applicable, perhaps with some modification for wood, to all of them.

There are 122 jacks in the harpsichord, two jacks for every note on the keyboard. As noted earlier, each jack consists of eight different parts. Each of these parts must be fitted together accurately so they will function properly when plucking and dampening the strings. Consequently, great care must be taken to machine and assemble all of these parts into a working jack. Each machining operation must be repeated 122 times. To do this machining accurately, special jigs are required and must be adapted to the specific tool being used. In the construction of the harpsichord illustrated in the frontispiece, a small, multipurpose tool known as a "Unimat" was used to machine the jacks. (The Unimat is a tool, similar to a watchmaker's lathe, that, with its accessories, can be used for precision sawing, milling, and drilling. As a result the jigs and instructions for their use are for this tool. Little difficulty should be experienced in adapting these jigs and instructions to other types of tools.)

The first step in the construction of the jacks is to cut out the blanks for the jack bodies from a sheet of plastic. In Figure 42 it can be seen that the finished dimensions of these blanks should be $3/16'' \times 1/2'' \times 4\ 3/8''$. One hundred and twenty-two of these bodies will require a sheet of 3/16-inch plastic measuring $18'' \times 27''$. Actually, 144 blanks can be cut from a sheet this size, which provides about 20 percent more blanks than needed. The extras can be used to replace those that are spoiled by accident during the various machining operations.

Begin forming the jack body blanks by truing one edge of the sheet of plastic on the jointer. Set the fence of a table saw fitted with a thin-rim veneer blade (at least 120 teeth for a 6-inch diameter blade) to exactly 1/2 inch and cut off the first strip. Deburr the edge of the strip with 8/0 garnet paper and trial-fit the strip into a slot in one of the jack slides. The strip should make a sliding fit in the slot with very little play. It should slide up and down easily but not rattle. Readjust the fence as necessary. Rejoint the edge of the sheet of plastic and saw off a second strip. Continue this process until all of the strips have been cut.

After all of the strips are cut, clamp a stop block to the miter gauge of the saw and cut the strips of plastic to 4 3/8-inch lengths.

Mount a $.031'' \times 2\ 1/2''$ metal-slotting saw blade on the saw arbor of the multipurpose tool. Adjust the fence on the saw table to remove a strip slightly less than 5/32 inch wide and 1 3/8 inches long from both sides of one end of the plastic blanks. A stop block can be clamped to the saw table to control the length of the cut. Make a cut on one side of the blank, turn the blank over and make a second cut on the opposite side. Repeat this process with all of the blanks. Remove the two strips from the blanks with a right-angle cut using a jig saw or a fine-toothed back saw. This should leave a

3/16-inch square section projecting from one end of the blank. It is preferable that this projection be slightly wider than 3/16 inch, rather than narrower. Later, this projection will be filed to fit the holes in the jack guide.

Set up a fence and stop block on the table of the jig saw and cut away the upper end of the jack blank so a projection 3/16 inch wide and 5/16 inch high remains as shown on the jack plan. Make the first cut lengthwise in the blanks and then turn the blanks 90 degrees and make the second cut

72. *Sawing the Jack Bodies*

crosswise. Set up a fence and stop block on the saw table of the multipurpose tool to cut the slot for the damper. This slot should be 1 inch long and centered 3/32 inch in from the long side of the blank.

Construct the jig shown in Figure 74. This jig is used to hold the blank while the slot for the jack tongue is machined. The jack-body blank is held in place by the cam. Pressure is applied to this cam with a strong rubber band. Set up the multipurpose tool for milling with a 1/4-inch-diameter routing bit or end mill in the chuck. Bolt the jig to the cross-slide, clamp a blank in the jig, and locate the routing bit so the slot will be cut 3/32 inch in from the short side. Make two pencil marks on the jig 1 1/8 inches apart to indicate the length each slot is to be cut. Do not attempt to cut the slot all the way through the blank with one pass. Instead, make several successive cuts 1/16 inch or less in depth.

An alternative way to cut the slots in

73. *Cutting the Damper Slot*

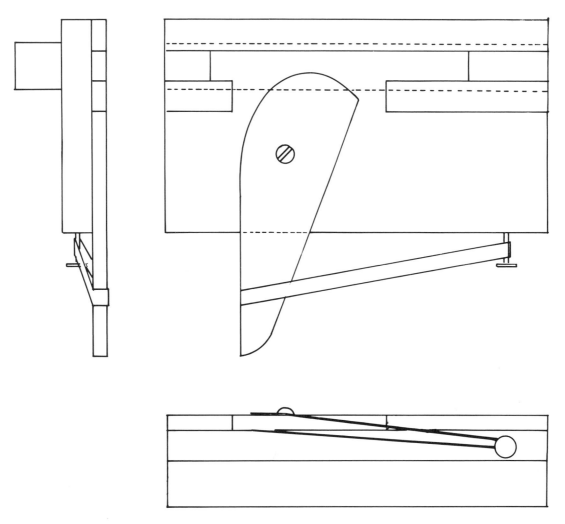

74. *Jig for Routing the Tongue Slot*

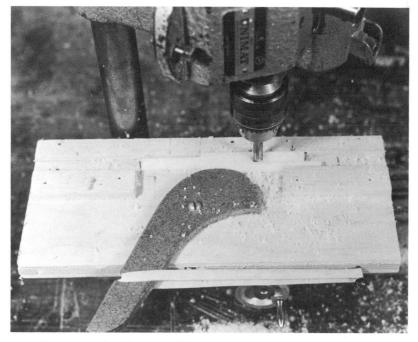

75. *Routing the Tongue Slot*

the jack bodies is to drill a 1/4-inch-diameter hole at each end of the slot and cut the intervening material out with a jig saw or coping saw.

When the slots have been cut, the axle hole, tongue-adjusting screw hole, and end-pin hole must be drilled in each blank. A drilling jig must be constructed for this purpose as shown in Figure 76. Rabbet the edge of the jig accurately so the axle hole will be centered 1/16 inch in from the back edge. To determine which side of the jack body is the back, place a jack body down on the workbench with the end-pin projection pointing toward the viewer and the long side of the jack body on the right. The upper surface of the jack body in this position is the back. Position and bolt the jig to the cross-slide of the multipurpose machine and use a 3/64 inch diameter drill bit to bore the axle holes.

Remove the drilling jig from the cross-slide and rerabbet the edge of the jig so the end-pin hole and the tongue-adjusting screw holes will be centered 3/32 inch in from either side of the blank. Rebolt the jig on the cross-slide and drill the end-pin holes 1/2 inch deep with a #50 drill bit. Reposition the jig and drill the tongue-adjusting screw holes with the same drill bit.

Convert the multipurpose tool into a drill-press configuration (or use a drill press). Put a 1/32-inch drill bit in the chuck. Reposition the drilling jig to drill the spring hole in the jack bodies where shown in Figure 42. Use very light pressure in drilling these holes, since the drill bit is very fragile.

Thread the end-pin holes and tongue-adjusting screw holes with a 2–56 tap. The fastest way to thread these holes is to chuck the tap in a hand drill. However, care must be taken to hold the drill steady when tapping, since the tap is very small and brittle, and can break quite easily. Do not attempt to tap the full length of the hole with one pass. Instead, run the tap in about 1/8 inch, then back it out to clear the chips, run the tap in another 1/8 inch, back the tap out, and repeat this process until the hole is tapped its entire length.

Sand the edges of the jack body and the inside of the slot for the tongue with #280 emery paper followed by #400 and #600 emery paper. Using a smooth-cut file, round the corners of the end-pin projection so it will just slip through the holes in the jack guide without binding. Be careful not to remove too much material or the jack will rattle in its guide.

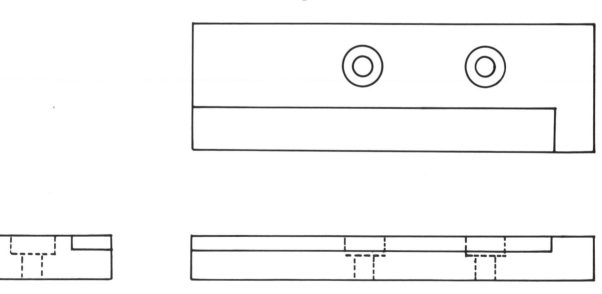

76. *Jig for Drilling the Jack Bodies*

When all of the jack bodies have been completed, the jack tongues can be made. The construction of the jack tongues will depend, in part, upon the type of plectra to be used in the harpsichord. If flat plastic plectra are to be used, then slots 1/50″ × 3/32″ must be formed in the tongues. If leather plectra are to be used, then square holes 3/32″ × 3/32″ must be formed in the tongues. It is very difficult to develop a technique whereby the slots for the plastic plectra can be formed by hand. Consequently, it is recommended that commercially available tongues for these plectra be purchased if this is the type desired. In the discussion that follows, instructions will be given for making tongues that use leather plectra.

The tongues are cut from 1/8″ × 3/16″ strips of plastic to the dimensions and shape shown in Figure 42. Cut the strips using the same general procedures described for cutting the jack body planks.

77. *Drilling the Jack Bodies*

Make a wooden miter box to the dimensions given in Figure 78. Place a strip of plastic in the slot of the miter box, tightly against the stop block. Cut the strip off to the correct length and then cut the bevel on the upper end. Repeat this process until a sufficient number of tongues have been cut. Be sure to make 10 or 15 extra tongues to allow for errors and accidents.

Bolt the jack-drilling jig on the cross-slide of the multipurpose tool and drill the axle hole in each tongue using a #55 drill bit. Refer to Figure 42 for the position of the axle hole. Reposition the drilling jig and drill the hole for the plectrum in each tongue with a 3/32-inch drill bit.

Pad the jaws of a small vise with masking tape. Clamp a tongue in the vise and square the sides of the plectrum hole with a 3/32-inch square needle file. Keep the sides of the hole parallel to the sides of the tongue and avoid enlarging the hole excessively. Repeat this operation with each of the tongues. Reclamp each tongue in the vise and

cut the groove for the spring in the back of each tongue with a small rattail file. Be careful not to cut the groove so deeply as to expose the axle hole. Complete the tongues by sanding them with #280, #400, and then #600 emery paper to remove any roughness on the edges and sides.

When the tongues have been completed, the jacks are ready for assembly. A 2-56 × 1/2″ roundhead machine screw is used for both the end pin and the tongue-adjusting screw. Drive the end-pin screw into its threaded hole so about 1/4 inch of it extends outside the hole. Drive the tongue-adjusting screw into its threaded hole so its tip barely extends into the tongue slot in the jack body. Repeat this procedure with each jack.

The jack spring is secured in place next. It is shaped as shown in Figure 42. Cut a 1 1/4-inch length of #2 (.011-inch) brass music wire. Use caution when handling the wire. Using a pair of needlenose pliers, make a sharp 90 degree bend and a 3/16-inch loop in one end of the wire. Insert the loop into

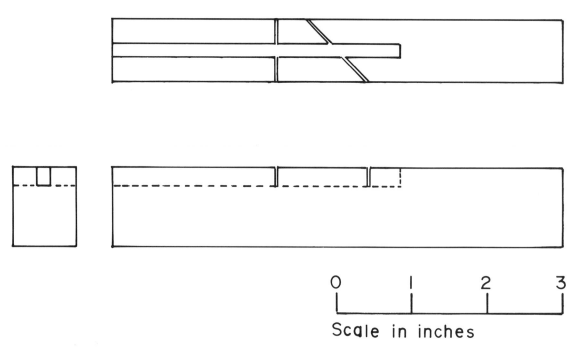

Scale in inches

78. *Miter Box for Cutting Jack Tongues*

the spring hole in the back of the jack (the back of the jack is the side that is nearest to the tongue-axle hole). Hold a small nail with a pair of pliers and heat the point over a flame. Press the hot point of the nail into the plastic of the jack body around the spring wire. This will melt the plastic and cause it to flow around the spring wire, holding it securely in place. Bend the upper end of the wire into a gentle outward curve. This curve prevents the spring wire from digging into the groove in the back of the tongue. Repeat the foregoing procedures with the remaining jacks.

Start a #18 1/2 center pin into the axle hole in the side of the jack body opposite the damper slot, the thinner of the two sides. The point of the pin should barely protrude into the tongue slot. Slip a tongue into this slot so the upper, beveled portion faces forward and the groove in the back faces the jack spring. Carefully align the axle hole in the tongue with the protruding tip of the center pin. Press the center pin through the tongue and into the axle hole on the opposite side of the slot. Tap the center pin through the jack body with a small hammer until its pointed end barely emerges from the jack body on the opposite side from where it was started. Check the action of the tongue in the slot to be sure it moves freely on the axle and does not bind against the sides or the ends of the slot in the jack body. The most usual problem encountered here is that the hole in the tongue may be bored at a slight angle rather than at a right angle to its sides. This will cause the tongue to sit crooked in the slot in the jack body. The simplest remedy is to replace the tongue. However, when the amount of bind is minimal, it sometimes is possible to file a small amount of material off the tongue where it binds against the side of the slot. This will free up the tongue's movement.

When satisfied with the fit of the tongue in the slot, cut off the excess length of the center pin and file its ends flush with the sides of the jack body. Adjust the jack spring so it presses against the groove in the tongue and forces the tongue slightly forward of the vertical. Screw the tongue-adjusting screw down until its end bears against the beveled surface of the tongue and stops its forward motion. The tongue should lie parallel to the jack body. Recheck the action of the jack spring. It should put enough tension on the tongue to press it lightly against the adjusting screw but not so much tension as to prevent the tongue from rotating back in its slot when pressed softly with the finger. Final adjustment to the spring tension will be made when the completed harpsichord is regulated.

The next step in the assembly of the jacks is fitting the plectra to the tongues. Directions are given here for leather plectra, although plastic plectra are fitted in a similar fashion. The leather used for plectra is cowhide shoe-sole leather. The leather is prepared by cutting it into square strips slightly wider and thicker than the plectra holes in the tongues. Begin by cutting the leather into strips that are the proper width for the hole in the tongue. Each strip is then thinned down to the proper thickness, leaving the hard, tanned portion on the strip. Once the strips have been cut, take one of the strips, cut the lower edge at a slight angle, and insert the end into the plectrum hole of one of the jacks from the back so the tanned surface is uppermost in the opening. Grasp the protruding leather from the front of the tongue with a pair of needlenose pliers and pull the leather through until it is firmly seated in the tongue. With a sharp knife, cut the leather so it is flush with the back of the tongue. Cut the leather off on the front side so only about 3/16 inch remains protruding from the tongue. Fit the remaining plectra in the same way. Their final shaping will take place during the voicing of the completed harpsichord.

Constructing the Stop Mechanism

The hand-stop mechanism controls the movement of the two jack slides and the harp stop. The mechanism consists of (1) the cam assembly, (2) the hand-stop assembly, and (3) the cable assembly. Complete drawings and specifications for the mechanism are given in Figures 22 and 24.

The cam bodies should be cut from 3/8-inch-diameter brass rod. One cam body should be 1 1/4 inches long; the other two cam bodies are each 1 inch long. Cut the three lengths of brass rod with a hacksaw and use a file to square and smooth the ends.

Cut three cam levers from 14-gauge sheet brass with a jeweler's saw to the shape shown in the drawings. Do not finish-file or drill the holes in these levers until after they are soldered to the cam bodies.

Place one of the cam bodies upright on an asbestos or charcoal soldering block. Coat the top surface of the cam body with silver soldering flux. Place three or four small pieces of silver solder on the flux and heat the brass with a torch until the solder melts and flows. Place a cam lever on the soldering block and give it a coat of flux. Place the cam body solder-end down on top of the cam lever. Position the two parts accurately, heat them with a torch until a bead of solder can be seen all around the joint between the cam body and the cam lever, remove the torch, and place the soldered cam in pickle to remove the flux and fire scale. Cut the edges of the cam lever flush with the cam body, and round off all the corners with a file. Repeat the above procedures with the remaining two cams.

Locate and center punch the position of the cam-screw axle hole on each cam. Note that the axle hole for the back jack slide (one of the one-inch cam bodies) is located toward the top edge of the cam when viewed with the cam lever pointing to the left, while the other two axle holes are located toward the bottom edges when the cam bodies are viewed in the same way. These axle holes must be accurately located in the position shown. Clamp each cam body in a drill-press vise, position it, and drill the cam-screw axle hole with a 9/64-inch drill bit.

Locate, center punch, and drill the hole for the clevis in each cam lever where shown. Use a #42 bit to drill these holes. Deburr the holes with a small rattail file.

The three cam followers are made from 5/8″ × 2″ rectangles of 14-gauge sheet brass. A slot 1/8 inch wide and 3/4 inch long should be cut in one end of each rectangle, and an opening rectangular in shape measuring exactly 1/2 inch wide and 3/8 inch long should be cut in the opposite end as shown. Use a jeweler's saw to cut the slots and openings. Smooth the edges with a flat smooth-cut file, and polish the cam followers with emery paper and fine steel wool.

Constructing the Hand-Stop Assembly. The hand-stop assembly consists of three control rods, each of which fits inside a guide tube. The guide tubes, in turn, are fastened to the nameboard. The following instructions are for one guide tube and control rod. Two additional guide tubes and control rods must be made. Most of the parts specified are used in lamp repair and can be obtained from a hardware store or lamp-repair shop. The thin-wall tubing can be purchased from a hobby shop.

Soft solder a 2-inch length of 9/32″ OD × 1/4″ ID thin-wall brass tubing inside a 2″ × 1/8″ brass-pipe nipple. The tubing serves to reduce the inside diameter of the pipe to a sliding fit for the 1/4-inch-diameter control rod. Clamp the brass nipple in the vise of the multipurpose tool. With a 3/16-inch-diameter end mill, cut a slot through one wall of the pipe for a distance of 1 inch. Thread a 3/4-inch knurled brass nut on the end of the nipple opposite the slot and soft solder it in place so it is flush with the end of the nipple. Be careful not to get solder on the outside face of the nut, for this would mar its appearance.

Cut a 2-inch length of 1/4-inch-diameter brass rod and drill a 3/32-inch-diameter hole 3/4 inch deep in one end of the rod. At the opposite end, drill a hole 3/4 inch deep with a #29 drill bit and thread the hole with an 8–32 tap. Start an 8–32 × 1 1/4″ brass machine screw into this hole and drive it to a binding fit. Cut the head off of the screw and clear any fouled threads with a small file.

Form a stud by filing a 1/4-inch-radius groove across the end of a 3/16-inch-diameter brass rod with a rattail file. Cut the stud off 1/4 inch from the end of the rod and silver solder it in place where shown on the end of the control rod. Clamp the control rod in a drill press vise with the stud projecting upward. Center a #43 drill bit over the stud and bore a hole completely through the stud and control rod. Thread the hole with a 4–40 tap. Start a 4–40 roundhead brass machine screw into the hole. Repeat the above procedures for the other two hand stops.

The installation of the hand-stop assembly in the nameboard is deferred until final assembly. At that time three 3/4-inch brass knobs, three additional 3/4-inch knurled brass nuts, three hexagonal brass nuts, and three brass washers will be needed.

Constructing the Cable Assembly. The cable and cable housings used in the hand-stop mechanism are short lengths of the same cable and cable housing used for the brake controls on bicycles. They may be purchased from any bicycle-repair shop. The clevises that are soft soldered to one end of each of the three cables are of the type used on the control rods of radio-controlled model airplanes and can be purchased at most hobby shops. Be sure to obtain the solder-type clevises, rather than the threaded type.

If desired for aesthetic reasons, the plastic covering of the cable housing can be stripped off with a knife and the inner metal coil can be slid into a brass tube of the appropriate inside diameter. Form the brass tubing to the curve shown in Figure 24 after the inner coil is in place.

The brackets for the control-cable assembly are made from 16-gauge sheet brass to the shape shown. Drill 3/42-inch holes through the upright arm of each bracket where the cables are to pass. Silver solder 1/2-inch lengths of brass tubing to the upright arms where shown to serve as sockets for the cable housing. Again, the tubing must be selected to fit the particular cable housing being used. Drill holes in the lower arm of each bracket as indicated with a #28 drill. (The brackets will be fastened to the wrest plank with #6 × 3/4″ roundhead brass wood screws during installation.) Smooth the edges of the brackets with a flat smooth-cut file and polish them with emery paper and fine steel wool.

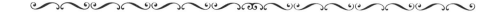

PART IV.

The Final Assembly of the Harpsichord

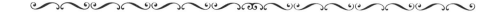

Once the case has been completely assembled and finished, the pins can be installed in the bridge, nut, and hitch-pin rail. Clear the bridge-pin holes in the bridge of any accumulated debris with a drill bit the same size as originally used to drill the holes. Wrap a small piece of masking tape around the drill bit to serve as a depth gauge so each hole can be cleared to the full depth needed in order for the bridge pins to project a scant 1/8 inch above the top of the bridge when driven in. Chuck the bit in a hand drill and run it in and out of each hole. Brush away the debris as it clears the hole so it will not fall back into another hole.

The bridge pins are driven in with a small hammer. A block of wood 1/8-inch thick is held alongside the pins as they are being driven to serve as a stop and to insure that all of the pins extend the same distance above the bridge. When driving the pins, use a series of light taps rather than heavy blows to avoid damage to the bridge or soundboard. After all of the bridge pins have been driven in, run a flat, smooth-cut file across their tops to even out any discrepancies in height. Follow this filing by passing a piece of emery paper wrapped around a small wooden block back and forth across the tops of the bridge pins to remove any burrs. Carefully brush away the metal filings so the small bits of metal do not become embedded in the wood of the bridge and soundboard. Repeat the foregoing procedures to install the pins in the nut and hitch-pin rail.

Installing the Hand-Stop Mechanism

The hand stops should be fitted to the wrest plank and nameboard as shown in Figures 22 and 24. Care must be taken in locating and drilling the lead holes for the cam-axle screws to insure their proper alignment with the jack slides. Use a #47 drill bit and #6 roundhead brass wood screws for the cam axles and for

mounting the cable-assembly brackets to the wrest plank.

Cut a slot in the bass end of the jack slide nearest the wrest plank and in the treble end of the other jack slide. The slot should be 1/8 inch wide and 3/4 inch long, centered in each slide as shown.

Drill two holes in the opposite end of each jack slide where shown with a #43 drill bit. Thread these holes with a 4-40 tap. Fasten the cam followers to the jack slides with 4-40 × 1/4″ roundhead brass machine screws. Place the jack slides in the wrest plank gap. Insert the short cam through the rectangular opening in the cam follower of the back jack slide. Insert a #6 × 1 1/2″ roundhead brass wood screw in the axle hole in the cam and drive it into the hole in the block in the wrest-plank gap. Repeat this procedure with the second jack slide and cam using a #6 × 2″ roundhead brass wood screw.

Equally space the free ends of the jack slides in the wrest-plank gap and mark the position for the hold-down screws where shown. Drill the lead holes for the two screws with a #49 drill bit. Drive a #5 × 1″ roundhead brass wood screw into each hole and tighten it snugly but not so tightly as to prevent the free lateral movement of the jack slides.

Place the harp batten on the wrest plank and secure it in position with the three screws used earlier. Attach the cam follower to the harp batten with two #6 × 3/8″ roundhead brass wood screws where shown. Fasten the cam to the wrest plank in the same way as those for the jack slides were mounted.

Fasten the control-cable assembly on the wrest plank using #6 × 3/4″ roundhead brass wood screws. Be sure that the cable housing for the harp-stop cam does not interfere with the tuning pins. Rebend the cable housing if necessary.

Install the hand-stop guide tubes through the holes in the nameboard with the soldered knurled nut on the outside. Slip a brass washer over each tube and tighten the tubes in place with the hexagonal nuts. Thread a second knurled nut onto the inner end of the three guide tubes.

Slide the control rods into the guide tubes with the small 4–40 machine screw and stud riding in the slot. Screw the brass knobs on the outer end of the control rod.

Slip the control cables into the cable housings from the cam end. The cable should be just long enough, so when the clevises are connected to the cams, the opposite end of the cable will reach about 1/2 inch into the end of the control rod. This measurement should be made when the control knobs are pushed all the way in and the cam levers are pointing at an angle of approximately 45 degrees toward the tail of the harpsichord. The cables are held in place in the end of the control rods with the 4–40 machine screws.

The travel of the jack slides can be adjusted in two ways. First, the screws holding the cam follower to the jack slide can be loosened and the slide relocated nearer or farther from the cam. Second, the knurled nut on the hand-stop guide tube can be turned nearer or farther from the end and thus controls the length of travel of the control rod, which, in turn, controls the travel of the cam lever and, ultimately, the travel of the jack slide. Coarse adjustments should be made by repositioning the cam follower on the slide, and fine adjustments by turning the knurled nut on the guide tube.

Stringing the Harpsichord

The stringing of the harpsichord requires the following items: (1) the string list, (2) a coil of music wire for each of the sizes given on the string list, (3) tuning pins, (4) a tuning wrench (also called a tuning hammer), (5) a small hammer, and (6) diagonal or other wire-cutting pliers. A few words of caution: The cut ends of music wire are very sharp and can easily puncture the skin. This danger is in-creased by the stiffness of the wire, which may cause short lengths to fly in unexpected directions when cut. Therefore, be very careful when handling music wire.

The stringing of the harpsichord can be started at either the treble or bass side of the instrument. Although the following instructions begin at the treble side, they are applicable in either case:

Consult the string list (Table 6) to determine the wire gauge to be used on the first pair of strings. Uncoil sufficient wire to reach from one tuning pin, across the nut and bridge to the hitch-pin rail, and back to a second tuning pin, with a foot or two of extra length. Insert the end of the wire through the hole in a tuning pin, allowing the wire to extend a half inch or so on the opposite side. Holding the tuning pin with the fingers, roll it in a clockwise direction until about six turns have been made (the square end of the tuning pin should point to the right). Holding the coils tightly on the tuning pin, tilt the pin and start it into the proper hole in the wrest plank. Drive the tuning pin in about 3/4 inch with the hammer. Keeping tension on the wire, snake it past the left side of the pin on the nut, the left side of the pin on the bridge, and around the first hitch pin in a counter-clockwise direction; then retrace the wire's path around the left side of the second bridge pin and second pin on the nut. Cut the wire off so it extends about three inches beyond the second tuning-pin hole. Insert the end of the wire in a second tuning pin, wind up, and drive it into its hole in the same way as described for the first tuning pin. Place the tuning wrench on the second tuning pin and tighten the string just enough to take out excess slack. Adjust the coils on the tuning pins so none overlap and all present a uniform appearance. Repeat with the coils on the first tuning pin. Tighten both strings just enough to prevent them from slipping out of position. Repeat the above procedures for each of the remaining sets of strings, changing wire sizes as indicated on the string list.

Installing the Jack Guide

The jack guide is fitted to the harpsichord after the strings have been installed but before the keyboard is fastened permanently in place. Locate the position of the jack guide within the harpsichord case underneath the wrest plank. Temporarily secure the jack guide in position with small pieces of double-faced tape. Put a jack in the last slot at the bass end of one of the jack slides and another jack in the last slot at the treble end. Move the jack slide sideways until the two jacks are centered between each set of strings. Check the jacks to be sure that they stand vertically between the strings. If they do not, reposition the jack guide. Once the jack guide is in proper alignment, the position of the screws can be marked, pilot holes can be drilled, and the jack guide fastened permanently in place. Replace the keyboard and secure it in place with four #8 × 1 1/4″ flathead steel wood screws.

Tuning the Harpsichord

When all of the strings have been fitted to the harpsichord, the process of bringing the instrument up to pitch can begin. The strings of the instrument are brought up to pitch through a series of gradual increases in tension. This helps the strings to stretch and the harpsichord to adjust to changes in tension and stress. If the instrument is brought up to pitch too suddenly, damage may occur to the soundboard and its bracing. The first rough tuning of the instrument should be at about one octave below its final pitch. Do not begin by tuning one octave to the desired pitch and then moving to another octave; rather, tune a particular pair of strings first and then tune the same pair of strings in the remaining octaves. In this way, tension will be applied gradually across the whole instrument rather than be concentrated in a single area. Since the jacks are not in position at this time, it will be necessary to pluck the strings with the fingers while tuning in order to determine their pitch.

Some standard will be needed against which the pitch of a specific string can be checked. A piano or similar keyboard instrument is ideal for this purpose. Lacking this, a chromatic pitch pipe or set of tuning forks can be used to tune the strings in a central octave and the strings in the remaining octaves can be checked against them.

It is difficult to describe in words the sound of a string being pulled up to pitch. However, the following description should serve as a guide: With the tuning wrench firmly seated on the tuning pin of the string to be tuned and the hand on top of the wrench rather than at the end (Figure 79), sound the proper note on the piano or other sound source, pluck the string to be tuned, and gradually turn the tuning pin in a clockwise direction with the tuning wrench. The sound of the string being tuned will begin by being obviously flat and will gradually increase in pitch until it sounds exactly the same as the pitch of the sound source. Then, if the tuning pin continues to be turned, the string will increase in pitch until it sounds obviously sharp. It is at this latter point, of course, that the string being tuned may break. Gradually loosen and tighten the string while it and the sound source are vibrating, and you will hear a series of vibrating sounds, a kind of "wow" "wow" "wow". These sounds are called "beats." They begin being heard as a rapid series when the pitch of the string is quite flat or quite sharp in comparison to the sound source. The speed of the beats slows down as the pitch comes closer to being identical to the sound source. In fact, the beats will become so slow that they can easily be counted (a phenomenon that will be used later in fine tuning the harpsichord). As the beats become slower and slower, they reach a point where they disappear. At this point the string is in perfect unison with the sound source; that is, they both are vibrating at the same frequency.

The beating phenomenon just described is not restricted simply to unisons but also will occur when strings are tuned to octaves, fifths, fourths, thirds, and other partials. This fact is used to advantage during the fine tuning of the harpsichord.

Once the first string of a pair has been tuned to the desired frequency, the second string is tuned in unison with it. That is, the tuned string is used as the standard to which the second string is tuned. When both strings have been rough-tuned in this way, they should be rechecked against the original sound source and any large errors in tuning should be corrected. It is not necessary to be extremely precise at this stage of tuning, since there will be rather large shifts in the pitch of various strings as the tuning process continues.

Once a pair of strings has been tuned, the pair of strings an octave below can be tuned to them, being careful to remain an octave below rather than tuning to the unison—which is easy to do and which frequently results in a broken string. Continue tuning by moving to the pair of strings an octave above and tuning them—tuning lower then higher octaves until all have been tuned.

After the octaves of the first pair of strings have been rough-tuned, the next pair of strings either directly above or below the original pair is tuned as described above. This process is continued until all of the strings have been rough-tuned.

Let the harpsichord rest for a few days and then retune, this time at a slightly higher pitch. Continue to tune, rest, tune, rest, until the harpsichord is brought to final pitch.

Because of the nature of its construction, the harpsichord needs frequent tuning. Under ideal conditions, with both temperature and humidity remaining constant, the instrument will need tuning at least every three weeks and, of course, immediately before any concert. Therefore, it is important that the harpsichord owner knows how to tune the instrument. This is not a very complicated task, and the novice should not be deterred from learning the skills required. With practice, almost anyone can become competent at tuning a harpsichord.

The fine tuning of the harpsichord is done after the jacks have been installed and regulated. There are three basic ways in which this fine tuning can be accomplished. They are, in descending order of cost: (1) to purchase an electronic device, such as the Conn Strobotuner, which allows each string of the instrument to be tuned accurately through visual rather than aural means; (2) to purchase an electronic or chromatic set of tuning forks, using these forks as standards to tune the middle octave of the harpsichord, and then tuning the other octaves in unison to this octave; and (3) to purchase a single tuning fork (usually C = 523), setting Pitch C with this tuning fork as a standard, and proceeding to tune the rest of the octave through the phenomenon of beats. It is this last process that is discussed in the section which follows.

The fine tuning is begun by first checking the rough tuning with a piano or similar sound source to be sure that the instrument is in approximate pitch throughout its entire range. This rough tuning is necessary so there will be no abrupt changes of tension imposed on the instrument during fine tuning. Such changes can affect the accuracy of any fine tuning that already has been done. Also, rough tuning the harpsichord helps the beginner to tune a given string to its proper pitch rather than to some other pitch that might "sound right".

During fine tuning, one set of strings is tuned across its entire range and the second set is match-tuned to the first set. Begin fine tuning by setting Pitch C (c^2) using the tuning fork as a standard. There should be no beats heard. Next, tune Middle C (c^1) to Pitch C ex-

79. *Manner of Holding Tuning Wrench*

cept an octave lower. Again, no beats should be heard. Fine tuning then progresses from Middle C up a fifth to G, then down a fourth to C, etc. Fifths are tuned slightly sharp (about .6 beats per second); fourths are tuned slightly flat (about .9 beats per second). A second can be approximated by saying the phrase "one thousand one" at a normal speaking rate. Thus, a fifth should have about one beat every two seconds, a fourth about one beat every second. The beat rate is changed, of course, by slightly altering the string tension by turning the tuning pin with the tuning wrench. Proceed to tune by fifths and fourths according to the following pattern:

c^1 up to g^1
g^1 down to d^1
d^1 up to a^1
a^1 down to e^1
e^1 up to b^1
b^1 down to b (tune octaves beatless)
b up to $f^{\#1}$
$f^{\#1}$ down to $c^{\#1}$
$c^{\#1}$ up to $g^{\#1}$
$g^{\#1}$ down to $d^{\#1}$
$d^{\#1}$ up to $a^{\#1}$
$a^{\#1}$ down to $a^{\#}$
$a^{\#}$ up to f^1
f^1 down to c^1

The procedure to use in tuning is to play the first note in the series, c^1, and while holding that key depressed play the second note in the series, g^1. With both notes sounding, turn the tuning pin for g^1 slightly until the proper beating rate is achieved, about one-half beat per second. At this point the tuning wrench should be carefully removed from the tuning pin to avoid disturbing the string's setting. When the last note in the octave, f^1, has been tuned, it should beat at the proper rate in relation to c^1, that is, .9 beats per second. If it does not, the tuning will have to be rechecked note for note until this beat rate is achieved. Do not disturb the setting of c^1 at any time during this process, for it provides the standard against which the remaining notes are tuned.

When the middle octave has been tuned satisfactorily, then the remaining octaves for that set of strings are tuned in relation to this octave, striving always for beatless octaves. When the first set of strings has been tuned satisfactorily, then the second set of strings is tuned in unison to the first. This completes the fine tuning of the instrument.

Installing, Voicing, and Regulating the Jacks

The installation of the jacks should begin with the farthest rank at the treble end. Select a jack and turn in the tongue-adjusting screw a couple of revolutions so the tongue lies slightly behind the vertical. (This is a precaution—in case the tip of the plectrum accidentally should be cut too short, the tongue can be advanced to the vertical and the plectrum recut.) Insert the jack in the first slot in the jack slide. Check the relationship between its plectrum and the string it will pluck. The plectrum should lie approximately 1/16 inch below the string. If the plectrum is too high, the end pin must be screwed in further. If the plectrum is too low, the end pin must be backed out slightly.

Check the distance the plectrum extends beyond the string with the stop for that rank of jacks in the on position. It should extend about 1/32 inch past the string. If the plectrum is too long, it must be cut off to the proper length at the angle shown in Figure 11. Note that the angle of cut for the leather plectrum is much less acute than that for the Delrin plectrum. To cut the plectrum, a sharp, thin-bladed knife and a hardwood block about 1/2″ × 1″ × 3″ will be needed. Hold the jack body upside down and flush against the block so the plectrum rests against the end grain of the piece of wood. Hold the knife at the desired angle and cut off the tip at the correct length. Check the action of the plectrum by depressing the key several times in rapid succession. The plectrum should pluck the string each time. Repeat the process, only this time release the key very, very slowly. In each instance the jack should fall back promptly, and the plectrum should slip past the string without hesitation. If the plectrum hangs on the string or the jack comes to a stop while the plectrum is still above the string, the difficulty may be a key that binds. Remove the jack from the jack slide and check the action of the key. Depress and release it slowly several times. It should drop back promptly when released. If it does not the problem is either binding against one of the two pins—in which case one or both of the holes in the key may have to be enlarged—or the key may be rubbing against one of its neighboring keys—in which case one of the two keys must be thinned slightly on the side where they rub together.

If, after this check of the key, the plectrum still hangs on the string, gently press the string out of the way and recheck the action of the jack, for it may be binding in the slot in the jack slide or in the hole in the jack guide. If this is the case, the proper remedy is to thin the area of the jack where it is binding. Usually, slightly rounding the corners of the jack remedies this problem. Be cautious in this operation to avoid removing so much material from the jack body as to cause it to become loose and rattle in the jack slide or guide.

If the jack moves freely but the plectrum still persists in hanging on the string, examine the action of the tongue and jack spring as the key is released slowly. It is possible that, as the plectrum presses the tongue backward in passing the string, some portion of the tongue or jack spring is binding against the jack slide. The correction for this problem usually is apparent and may range from rebending the spring slightly to enlarging the central opening in the slot of the jack slide. If the jack does not bind in the slide, then there may be too much tension exerted against the tongue by the jack spring. Bending the spring slightly away from the tongue will decrease its tension.

If neither the tongue nor the spring seems to be causing the difficulty, the problem probably is with the plectrum. It may lie too close under the string, in which case the end pin must be turned in farther. If the trouble still persists, the plectrum may be rough on the underside of the bevel cut. Check and remove any roughness either by making a very thin second cut on the tip or by smoothing the surface with a piece of extra-fine emery paper that has been glued to a small piece of wood so it can be used like a file. If the jack still persists in hanging on the string, the plectrum is too long and merely must be cut shorter.

It may be discovered in checking the action of the jack that the plectrum fails to pluck on occasion. There are several possible causes here, the most serious of which is that a jack fits too loosely in the jack slide or guide and, as a consequence, the jack changes its position forward and backward in the slot as the key is played. This movement affects the relationship of the plectrum to the string. A cure for a defect of this type is difficult to achieve, short of making a new jack body, if only this jack or a few jacks fit loosely. If all of the jacks are equally loose, the solution is either to make new jacks or new jack guides and slides. One solution, temporary at best, is to cut narrow strips of plastic tape and adhere them to the sides of the jack where the looseness occurs.

A more usual cause of the failure of a jack to pluck repeatedly is a plectrum that has been cut too short. In this case, turning the tongue-adjusting screw out a revolution or so may effect a cure. If the plectrum still is too short, a new plectrum must be installed in the tongue. Finally, failure of a jack to pluck repeatedly may be because the jack spring is too weak. This can be remedied by bending in the spring with a pair of tweezers so it is tighter against the tongue.

Once the action of the plectrum repeats well, attention can be given to voicing the plectrum. In voicing, the objective is to achieve a plucking sound that is clean and crisp with only a light touch of the key (Zuckermann in bibliographic reference 4 suggests that a 3 1/2-ounce weight placed on the key should cause the jack to pluck). The voicing of a leather plectrum requires the underside to be gradually thinned in a tapering cut until the desired sound and touch has been achieved. This tapering should be gradual from back to front, resulting in a shape similar to that shown in Figure 11. Remove only a small layer of leather at a time and check the results by replacing the jack in the harpsichord and depressing the key several times. If the touch is too heavy or the sound is too harsh, more leather must be removed from the underside of the plectrum.

The voicing of a Delrin plectrum follows the same procedures as those described for leather, except Delrin plectra may be thinned along the sides as well as on the bottom to achieve the desired touch and sound. Regardless of the type of plectra being used, a very sharp knife is essential during the voicing process.

Once the plectrum has been voiced, a 3/8″ × 3/8″ square piece of damper felt should be inserted in the damper slot and pulled downward until it just touches the string when the key is in the rest position. When this has been accomplished, the end pin of the jack should be turned in about one-half of a revolution so the jack actually hangs on the string with its damper rather than rests upon the key. The damper must be cut long enough so it will dampen the vibrations of the string in both the on and the off position, but it must not be so long that it touches the neighboring string in the on position. A knife and a cutting block are useful in trimming the damper to size.

Once the first jack has been satisfactorily adjusted and voiced, the subsequent jacks in the register can be installed and adjusted. The objective is to achieve a similar touch, tonal quality, and volume from each jack so the entire rank of jacks will sound uniform. Minor adjustments in volume can be achieved through the use of the tongue-adjusting screw.

The second rank of jacks is installed, voiced, and regulated in the same manner as the first. However, the end pins must be adjusted so the plectra of the jacks in this rank pluck just slightly earlier than the plectra of the jacks in the first rank. The reason for this staggered plucking order is to decrease the amount of effort needed to play the harpsichord. If both jacks were to pluck at exactly the same time, twice the amount of effort would be required to depress the key than if they were to pluck in sequence. During the voicing, both jacks for a given key should be adjusted so each produces about the same volume and has about the same touch. Of course, their tonal characteristics will be different, because the two jacks will pluck their respective strings at different plucking points, and, as a result, produce different harmonics.

Adjusting the Harp Stop

After all of the jacks have been installed, voiced, and regulated, attention can be given to adjusting the harp stop. Each of the damper pads should mute the strings to the same extent as their neighbors on either side. If there is considerable difference in the muting of the strings—that is, if some of the pads touch the strings firmly and some touch them lightly or not at all—it will be necessary to reset the on position of the harp stop, either with the fine-adjustment nut on the hand-stop guide tube or by loosening the screws holding the cam follower to the harp batten, moving the batten to the right or the left as necessary, and retightening the screws. Slight inequalities in the muting effect of an individual pad can be compensated for by bending the tab on which the pad is mounted to increase or decrease the pressure of the pad on the string.

When the foregoing adjustments and regulatings have been completed, the lid can be put back on the harpsichord and the hinge pins replaced. The construction of the harpsichord is finished and the instrument is ready to be played.

BIBLIOGRAPHY

Bessaraboff, Nicholas. *Ancient European Musical Instruments.* Harvard University Press, Cambridge, Mass., 1941.

Boalch, Donald. *Makers of the Harpsichord and Clavichord.* George Ronald, London, 1956.

Galpin, Francis. *A Textbook of European Musical Instruments.* Williams and Norgate, London, 1937.

Grove, George. *Dictionary of Music and Musicians.* Eric Blom, editor. Volumes 1–9, MacMillan, fifth edition, London, 1954.

Hipkins, A. J. *A Description and History of the Pianoforte and of the Older Keyboard Stringed Instruments.* Novello, London, 1896.

[1] Hubbard, Frank. *Harpsichord Regulating and Repairing.* Tuners Supply, Inc., Boston, 1967.

[2] Hubbard, Frank. *Three Centuries of Harpsichord Making.* Harvard University Press, Cambridge, Mass., 1965.

James, Phillip. *Early Keyboard Instruments.* Peter Davies, London, 1930.

Neupert, Hanns. *Harpsichord Manual, an Historical and Technical Discussion.* Translated from the German by F. E. Kirby. Barenreiter, New York, 1960.

[3] Russell, Raymond. *The Harpsichord and Clavichord.* Faber and Faber, London, 1959.

Sachs, Curt. *The History of Musical Instruments.* Norton, New York, 1940.

Zuckermann, Wolfgang Joachim. *The Modern Harpsichord.* October House, New York, 1969.

APPENDIX 1.

The English Notation System

g³	a³
e³	f³
c³	d³
a²	b²
f²	g²
d²	e²
b¹	c²
g¹	a¹
e¹	f¹
c¹	d¹

a	b
f	g
d	e
B	c
G	A
E	F
C	D
AA	BB
FF	GG
DD	EE
	CC

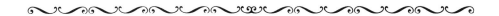

APPENDIX 2.

Fractional and Decimal Equivalents

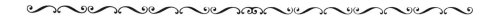

1/32	.03125	17/32	.53125
1/16	.0625	9/16	.56265
3/32	.09375	19/32	.59375
1/8	.12500	5/8	.62500
5/32	.15625	21/32	.65625
3/16	.18750	11/16	.68750
7/32	.21875	23/32	.71875
1/4	.25000	3/4	.75000
9/32	.28125	25/32	.78125
5/16	.31250	13/16	.81250
11/32	.34375	27/32	.84375
3/8	.37500	7/8	.87500
13/32	.40625	29/32	.90625
7/16	.43750	15/16	.93750
15/32	.46875	31/32	.96875
1/2	.50000	1	1.00000

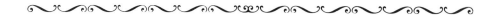

APPENDIX 3.

Plans for a Slotting Saw

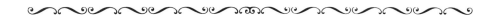

The saw used to cut the slots in the aluminum jack slides is constructed from readily available materials and includes the following parts: (1) a 3/16″ × 3″ metal-slotting saw blade with a 7/8-inch arbor hole, (2) a saw mandrel with a 7/8-inch-diameter arbor, (3) a 1/4 horsepower or 1/3 horsepower electric motor, and (4) a saw frame and table fitted with a miter gauge. The accompanying photographs (Figures 80, 81, 82, 83) illustrate the essential construction of the tool. No measurements are given, because they will vary according to the specific parts used in the construction of the saw.

The metal-slotting saw blade is a standard industrial item used with horizontal milling machines. It comes in a variety of widths and diameters, with arbor holes ranging from 7/8 inch upward. If a saw mandrel cannot be found with an arbor that is large enough, the difference in size between the arbor and the hole in the saw blade can be made up with an arbor insert that has the correct outside diameter to fit the hole in the saw

blade and the correct inside diameter to fit the saw-mandrel arbor.

Almost any small fractional-horsepower motor can be used to power the saw. The pulleys for the motor and saw-mandrel shafts should be selected to produce a cutting speed of about 800 feet per minute. For a 3-inch-diameter saw blade, this cutting speed translates into 1018 rpm. With a motor speed of 1750 rpm and a 3-inch drive pulley on the motor, a 1 3/4-inch pulley on the shaft of the saw mandrel will produce a blade speed of 1020 rpm.

The frame and miter gauge of the saw are constructed from wood, using simple butt joints. All parts of the saw frame should be fastened together with screws and glue to insure rigidity of construction. The height of the motor mount will be determined by the particular motor being used. It should be so mounted that the top of the V-belt falls below the top of the saw table so the belt will not interfere with the movement of the jack slides as they are being cut. Care should be taken in

80. *View of Slotting Saw*

81. *Slotting Saw Table*

82. *Underside of Miter Gauge*

83. *Slotting Saw with Table Removed*

cutting the slot for the miter gauge in the top of the fixed table to insure that it is parallel to the path of the saw blade. The miter gauge should be fitted with an aluminum bar or channel that will slide in this slot smoothly without side play. Waxing the table, slot, and bar will help to reduce friction.

The miter gauge stop is made from a 1/2-inch-wide strip of 14-gauge brass to which a stud made from 3/16-inch-diameter brass rod has been soldered. The stop controls the spacing of the slots in the jack slides. It pivots on the forward screw and is adjusted by loosening the rear screw and turning the center screw, which, because it has an eccen-

tric head, causes the stop to pivot to one side or the other. The eccentric screw is formed by turning an ordinary screw slightly off-center on a metal lathe or multipurpose tool. A gauge of wood or metal measuring exactly 1/3 inch (.3333 inch) can be used to set the stop in the correct relationship to the blade of the saw.

The saw mandrel is mounted to the frame with carriage bolts. The heads of these bolts are countersunk into the underside of the saw table. The table should be mounted to the frame so the blade of the saw projects 3/32 inch above its surface.

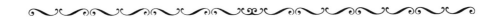

APPENDIX 4.

Decimal Equivalents of Fractional, Letter, and Number Drill Sizes

FRACTION	LETTER	NUMBER	DECIMAL
		80	.0135
		79	.0145
1/64			.0156
		78	.0160
		77	.0180
		76	.0200
		75	.0210
		74	.0225
		73	.0240
		72	.0250
		71	.0260
		70	.0280
		69	.0292
		68	.0310

FRACTION	LETTER	NUMBER	DECIMAL
1/32			.0312
		67	.0320
		66	.0330
		65	.0350
		64	.0360
		63	.0370
		62	.0380
		61	.0390
		60	.0400
		59	.0410
		58	.0420
		57	.0430
		56	.0465
3/64			.0469
		55	.0520
		54	.0550
		53	.0595
1/16			.0625
		52	.0635
		51	.0670
		50	.0700
		49	.0730
		48	.0760
5/64			.0781
		47	.0785
		46	.0810
		45	.0820
		44	.0860
		43	.0890
		42	.0935
3/32			.0937
		41	.0960
		40	.0980
		39	.0995
		38	.1015
		37	.1040
		36	.1065

FRACTION	LETTER	NUMBER	DECIMAL
7/64			.1094
		35	.1100
		34	.1110
		33	.1130
		32	.1160
		31	.1200
1/8			.1250
		30	.1285
		29	.1360
		28	.1405
9/64			.1406
		27	.1440
		26	.1470
		25	.1495
		24	.1520
		23	.1540
5/32			.1562
		22	.1570
		21	.1590
		20	.1610
		19	.1660
		18	.1695
11/64			.1719
		17	.1730
		16	.1770
		15	.1800
		14	.1820
		13	.1850
3/16			.1875
		12	.1890
		11	.1910
		10	.1935
		9	.1960
		8	.1990
		7	.2010

FRACTION	LETTER	NUMBER	DECIMAL
13/64			.2031
		6	.2040
		5	.2055
		4	.2090
		3	.2130
7/32			.2187
		2	.2210
		1	.2280
	A		.2340
15/64			.2344
	B		.2380
	C		.2420
	D		.2460
1/4	E		.2500
	F		.2570
	G		.2610
17/64			.2656
	H		.2660
	I		.2720
	J		.2770
	K		.2810
9/32			.2812
	L		.2900
	M		.2950
19/64			.2969
	N		.3020
5/16			.3125
	O		.3160
	P		.3230
21/64			.3281
	Q		.3320
	R		.3390
11/32			.3437
	S		.3480
	T		.3580

FRACTION	LETTER	NUMBER	DECIMAL
23/64			.3594
	U		.3680
3/8			.3750
	V		.3770
	W		.3860
25/64			.3906
	X		.3970
	Y		.4040
13/32			.4062
	Z		.4130
27/64			.4219
7/16			.4375
29/64			.4531
15/32			.4687
31/64			.4844
1/2			.5000

APPENDIX 5.
Tap Drill Sizes

NUMBER OR FRACTION	TAP		TAP-DRILL		DRILL FOR CLEARANCE
	NC	NF	NC	NF	
0		80		3/64	51
1	64	72	53	53	47
2	56	64	50	50	42
3	48	56	47	45	37
4	40	48	43	42	31
5	40	44	38	37	29
6	32	40	36	33	26
8	32	36	29	29	17
10	24	32	25	21	8
12	24	28	16	14	1
1/4	20	28	7	3	same as tap
5/16	18	24	F	1	same as tap
3/8	16	24	5/16	Q	same as tap
7/16	14	20	U	25/64	same as tap
1/2	13	20	27/64	29/64	same as tap

APPENDIX 6.
Clearance and Lead-Hole Sizes for Wood Screws

SCREW GAUGE	BODY HOLE	LEAD HOLE	SCREW GAUGE, INCHES
0	53		.060
1	49		.073
2	44	56*	.086
3	40	52*	.099
4	33	51*	.112
5	1/8	49*	.125
6	28	47	.138
7	24	46	.151
8	19	42	.164
9	15	41	.177
10	10	38	.190
11	5	37	.203
12	7/32	36	.216
14	D	31	.242
16	I	28	.268
18	19/64	23	.294

*In hardwoods only.

APPENDIX 7.
Sources of Materials

Harpsichord Action Parts

American Piano Supply Co.
Main Avenue and South Parkway
Clifton, New Jersey 07014
(music wire, tuning pins, key pins,
bridge pins, felts, tools)

Frank Hubbard Inc.
185A Lyman Street
Waltham, Massachusetts 02154
(jacks, tongues, plectra, kits)

Tuners Supply Co., Inc.
94 Wheatland Street
Somerville, Massachusetts 02145
(music wire, tuning pins, key pins,
bridge pins, felts, tools, jacks,
tongues, plectra)

Special Tools

Brookstone
127 Vose Farm Road
Peterborough, New Hampshire 03458

Woodcraft
313 Montvale Avenue
Woburn, Massachusetts 01801

Woods

Maurice Condon Co., Inc.
248 Ferris Avenue
White Plains, New York 10603
(spruce, hardwoods, plywood)

Constantine
2050 Eastchester Road
Bronx, New York 10461
(hardwoods, veneers, tools)

Craftsman Wood Service Co.
2729 South Mary Street
Chicago, Illinois 60608
(spruce, hardwoods, veneers, tools)

John Harra Wood and Supply Co.
39 West 19th Street
New York, New York 10011
(hardwoods, veneers)

North Hudson Woodcraft Corp.
Dolgeville, New York 13329
(custom soundboards)

Index

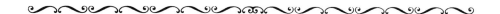